USBORNE
TIMELINES
OF
WORLD HISTORY

Jane Chisholm

Designed by Keith Newell, Mike Olley, Melissa Alaverdy, Robin Farrow & Julia Rheam
History consultant: Dr. Anne Millard

Cover design by Zöe Wray

Managing designer: Stephen Wright

Illustrated by Susanna Addario, Philip Argent, Gary Bines, Simone Boni, Stephen Conlin, David Cuzik, Peter Dennis, Luigi Galante, Jeremy Gower, Nicholas Hewetson, Ian Jackson, Colin King, John Lawrence, Joseph McEwan, Justine Torode, Evie Safarewicz, Claudia Saraceni, Ross Watton, Gerald Wood and David Wright

Map illustrations by Jeremy Gower

Contents

The Pyramids at Giza in Egypt, built in *c.2500BC*

How to use this book

This book is divided up into seven sections, with dates arranged in columns according to geographical area. This means you can look up what was happening in different parts of the world at the same time.

To help you put the dates in context, the columns also contain short features on important themes in world history, such as the Renaissance, or the Industrial Revolution.

Dates that appear in brackets after a person's name, such as Isaac Newton (1642-1727), refer to his or her life. In the case of kings, queens and emperors, such as Maria Theresa (1740-1780), the dates of the reign are shown instead.

Experts often disagree about dates in very early history, so you may find that some of dates shown are slightly different in other books.

Abbreviations

c. stands for *circa*, the Latin for "about". Early dates often begin with **c.** because experts have only been able to find an approximate date for when something happened.

AD stands for *Anno Domini*, meaning "Year of the Lord" in Latin. It applies to all the years after the birth of Jesus Christ, but it is normally only used with very early dates, to avoid confusion with **BC** dates.

BC means "Before Christ", and so **BC** dates are counted backwards from **AD** 1. However, many historians now believe that the year of Christ's birth was probably about 5BC, rather than the year 1.

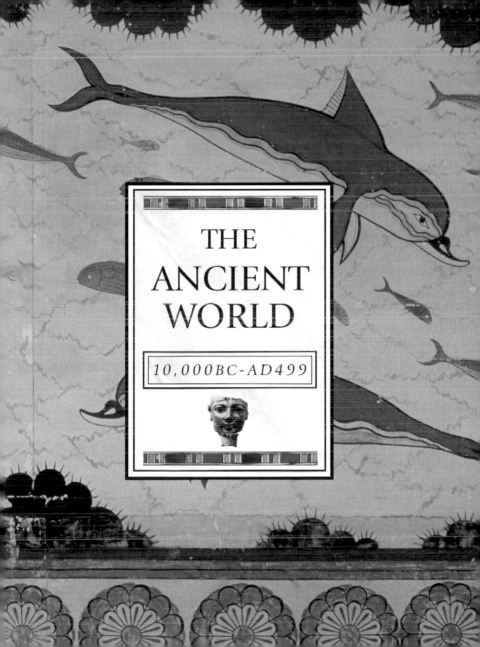

THE
ANCIENT
WORLD

10,000BC-AD499

Europe

THE FIRST ARTISTS

The world's first known artists were the Palaeolithic (Old Stone Age) people of Europe. Animal paintings, including bison, reindeer, horses and hunting scenes, dating back to **c.35,000-18,000BC**, have been found on the walls of caves in the Dordogne region of France, and the Pyrenees region of Spain.

Cave painting of a bison found at Lascaux, Dordogne, France

c.6000BC Groups of farmers, possibly from Turkey, reach Crete, mainland Greece and the Aegean islands.

c 6000-5000 A village is built at Lepenski Vir, on the banks of the Danube in central Europe.

c.6000-4000 Farming spreads throughout northern and western Europe.

c.4500-1500 Building of megaliths, large stone monuments such as temples, tombs and henges (circular areas, often made of stones), in Malta, Brittany, the Iberian peninsula (Spain and Portugal) and the British Isles.

c.4000 Copper is worked in the Balkans.

c.3800 The Sweet Track is built, one of the first walkways in England. It stretches for 1.8km (just over a mile).

c.3500 The first of several temples is built at Tarxien, Malta.

c.3200 Stone circles are built in north-western Europe.

c.3100 Skara Brae, a village in the Orkney Islands, is built from local stone.

c.3000-1500 Stone circle built at Stonehenge, Britain.

Stonehenge, the most spectacular of many megaliths in Britain

c.3000 Olives, vines and grains cultivated in the Aegean islands.

c.2500 Bronze, obsidian (volcanic glass) and flint are traded.

c.2500-2000 Corded Ware and Beaker cultures spread in northern Europe.

The Middle East

Wild goat

THE FIRST FARMERS

The earliest people lived as nomads, moving from place to place, hunting and eating wild plants. Farming probably first developed in about **10,000BC** in an area of the Middle East called the Fertile Crescent (see map). As people adopted farming, they began to build permanent places to live, and so the first towns grew up, such as Jericho and Çatal Hüyük (see below).

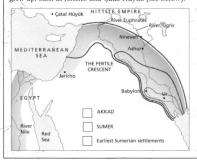

c.8000BC Jericho, in Jordan, has about 2,000 people.

c.7000 Pottery, spinning, weaving and hammering metal are in use.

c.6250-5650 Çatal Hüyük, in Turkey, has over 5,000 people.

c.4000 People learn to extract copper and gold.

MESOPOTAMIA

One of the world's earliest civilizations grew up in Mesopotamia, an area of fertile land between the rivers Tigris and Euphrates in what is now Iraq. Cities developed from about 4000BC, with impressive public buildings and organized political and legal systems. In southern Mesopotamia, known as Sumer, the wheel was invented, and a form of writing, known as cuneiform. Between 3100BC and 2800BC, small states were set up around the cities of Ur, Eridu and Uruk.

Gold dagger and sheath

Necklaces of gold and semi-precious stones

Treasures from the royal Sumerian tombs at Ur c.2500BC

c.3500 The wheel is invented in Sumer.

c.3300 The Sumerians develop writing.

c.2350-2150 The kingdom of Akkad is established in Mesopotamia.

c.2100BC Ur rules Sumer and Akkad. A ziggurat (a vast stepped tower with a temple on top) is built at Ur.

Africa

c.6000BC People in the Sahara Desert tame cattle.

c.5000 The Sahara Desert, once green, is still fertile in parts and there is evidence of cattle herders. As the Sahara continues to dry out, many people migrate to the Nile Valley.

c.5000 Farming begins in Egypt. Pottery, linen making and, later, metal working are developed.

c.4000 The Sahara grasslands have turned to desert.

ANCIENT EGYPT

The remarkable civilization of Ancient Egypt grew up along the banks of the great river, the Nile. By **c.3300**, the country was organized into two kingdoms: Upper and Lower Egypt, and the Egyptians developed a form of picture writing, which we call hieroglyphics. In **c.3100**, Upper and Lower Egypt were united by a king called Menes. The Ancient Egyptians produced fine works of art and architecture. They also demonstrated extraordinary feats of engineering, building the pyramids (see below) as tombs for their kings.

Egyptian hieroglyphs

c.2686-2181 Old Kingdom in Egypt: dynasties III to VI. The pyramids are built.

c.2180-2040 First Intermediate Period in Egypt: dynasties VII-X.

c.2040-1720 Middle Kingdom in Egypt: dynasties XI-XIII.

Pyramids and Sphinx at Giza, Egypt

Asia

c.9000-5000BC Jomon Period in Japan: people hunt and fish.

c.5000 Gradual adoption of farming in China. The Yangshao culture grows up around the Huang Ho River. Farmers grow millet, fruit, nuts and vegetables and keep pigs and dogs.

c.4000 Farming develops along the Yangtze River in China. Beginning of the cultivation of rice.

c.4000 Farming communities settle in the Indus Valley in India.

c.3000 Hunter gatherers living on Japanese islands. Use of pottery.

c.2700 Silk-making begins in China.

c.2500 Longshan period in China. Farmers are better organized and keep chickens, cattle, sheep, goats, and buffalo.

THE INDUS VALLEY CIVILIZATION

From **c.2300-1800**, the Indus Valley Civilization flourished in India, based on farming, with contacts as far west as Mesopotamia. The Indus Valley people had large cities, with public buildings and good sanitation, and a form of writing. The best known sites are Mohenjo Daro and Harappa.

Baked clay figure from Indus Valley

- Indus Valley civilization
- Empire of Chandragupta 297BC
- Expansion to 232BC under Asoka

Map showing early Indian empires

c.2500-1500 Bronze Age culture in Bactria, in Central Asia.

c.2205 Traditional earliest date of Xia (or Hsia) dynasty in China.

The Americas

c.15,000BC First people arrive in North America, crossing over from Asia via a bridge of land and ice.

Crossings were probably made over land bridges that appeared when the sea froze and water levels dropped

c.10,000-8000 Early North Americans hunt large animals.

c.8000-1000 North America: People spread out across plains, woodlands, deserts and icy wastes and gradually change from hunting to a more settled way of life.

c.5000 Corn farming in Central America.

Llama

c.3500 The llama is first used as a pack animal in Peru.

c.3200 Pottery is in use in Ecuador.

c.3000 Hunter gatherers known as Cochise are living in the southwest of North America.

c.2300 The introduction of farming leads to settlement in permanent villages in Mexico.

c.2300 Use of pottery spreads to Mexico and Guatemala.

Europe

c.2000BC Horses and wheeled vehicles are used in eastern Europe.

THE MINOANS

The earliest known European civilization developed in Crete between c.3000-2000BC. It is known as Minoan, after a legendary king called Minos. The Minoans had well-planned towns, skilled craftsmen and good trading links with the Mediterranean. Their golden age is known as the First and Second Palace Periods (c.2000-1700BC and c.1700-1450BC): they built large and spectacular palaces, including Knossos, Mallia and Phaistos. The Minoans introduced a form of writing, known as Linear A, from c.1650BC.

This bull's head is actually a vessel, called a rhyton. It was used for pouring liquid offerings to the gods.

c.2000-1500 Wessex culture in southern Britain.

THE MYCENAEANS

From c.1600-1200BC, Greece was dominated by people known as Mycenaeans, after Mycenae, the site where their remains were first discovered. They lived in small kingdoms, each based around a city, took over the prosperous Minoan trade routes, and developed Linear B, an early form of Greek writing, in c.1400BC.

c.1450 Volcanic eruption on Thera (an island near Crete).

c.1450 Fall of Knossos. Mycenaeans invade Crete.

c.1300 Bronze Age culture in central Europe, known as the Urnfield culture.

c.1250 Trojan Wars, between Mycenaeans and Trojans (from the city of Troy, in Turkey), end in the destruction of Troy.

Mycenaeans tricked the Trojans with the gift of a wooden horse, with soldiers hidden inside.

c.1200 Mycenaean cities are gradually abandoned.

c.1100-800 Dark Ages in Greece: Mycenaean civilization collapses, old cities are destroyed, people disperse and the art of writing is forgotten.

8

The Middle East

c.2000BC Hittite people arrive in Anatolia (Turkey).

BABYLON AND ASSYRIA

In c.2000BC, a desert tribe called the Amorites set up kingdoms around the old city-states of Mesopotamia. Two of these - Babylon and Assyria - grew into great empires. Under King Hammurabi (c.1792-1750BC), Babylon conquered Akkad and Sumer, and other territory. Hammurabi was also a great administrator, and was concerned for the welfare of his people.

Assyrian gold

The Assyrian kingdom was based around the cities of Ashur and Nineveh. The Assyrians were an aggressive, militaristic people. Under King Shamshi-Adad and his son, Ishme Dagan, the Assyrians built up their first empire (c.1814-1754BC).

Painting of an Assyrian official

c.1650-1450 Hittite Old Kingdom: Hittites set up small states in Turkey. They sack Babylon in c.1595.

c.1550-1200 Most of Canaan is ruled by Egyptians.

c.1500 Aryans settle in the land now called Iran.

c.1450 Assyrian empire is taken over by the Mitanni people.

c.1450-1200 Hittite New Kingdom: their territory stretches from the Mediterranean to the Persian Gulf.

c.1400 First mention in Egyptian records of groups of raiders, known as the Sea Peoples, in the Mediterranean.

A reconstruction of a sea battle between Egyptians and Sea Peoples, based on a carving at Luxor in Egypt

c.1375-1047 Middle Assyrian empire.

c.1300 Medes and Persians settle in Iran.

c.1250 Hebrews arrive in Canaan.

c.1200 Sea Peoples conquer Cyprus and Mediterranean cities, destroying most of the Hittite empire by c.1195.

c.1200-1000 Rise of Phoenicians in Lebanon. They found cities at Byblos, Sidon, Beirut and Tyre. Their alphabet forms the basis for Greek, Latin and modern Roman scripts.

c.1150 Peleset (or Philistines), a group of Sea Peoples, settle in Canaan, later called Palestine, after them.

c.1020 Saul becomes king in Israel.

c.1010-926 United Jewish kingdom of Israel.

Africa

c.1720BC
Egypt is invaded
by people called
the Hyksos.

Egyptian model of fishing boats, found in a tomb

c.1674-1567
2nd
Intermediate Period in Egypt:
dynasties XIV-XVII.

c.1600-1000 Egypt rules Kush
(Sudan).

THE NEW KINGDOM IN EGYPT

The Egyptian New Kingdom
(dynasties XVIII-XX) lasted from
c.1567-1085BC. This was the
period when Egypt's power was at
its height. Their warrior kings,
known as pharaohs, conquered a
vast empire, and were buried in
brightly decorated tombs, deep in
the cliff sides of the Valley of the
Kings, near Thebes.

Egyptian mummy

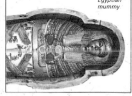

c.1500 Cattle and goats are
domesticated in West Africa.

1490-1468 Reign of
Hatshepsut, female
pharaoh
of Egypt.

Carved head of Hatshepsut

c.1450 Egyptian
empire reaches its
greatest extent.

1364-1347 Egypt: reign
of Akhenaten. He tries
to impose the worship of one god, but
fails.

c.1285 Battle of Quadesh between
Egypt and Hittites: neither side wins.

1280 Ramesses II of Egypt makes
peace with the Hittites.

1190 Ramesses III of Egypt defeats the
Sea Peoples.

c.1085 Nubia and Kush regain their
independence from Egypt.

1085-656 3rd Intermediate Period in
Egypt: dynasties XXI-XXV. Egypt
begins to decline.

Asia

c.1800BC The
Indus Valley
civilization starts
to decline, partly
due to the arrival of
Indo-Europeans, or
Aryans, from the
northwest from
c.1500, and partly to
the flooding of the
Indus, which
destroys cities
already in decline.
Aryan control
spreads as far east as
the Ganges river.

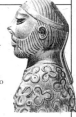

This statue may be of an Indus Valley ruler or priest.

c.1766-1027 First known
Chinese dynasty, the
Shang, rules China. A
feudal state, with walled
cities and temples ruled
by priest-kings.

The Bronze Age in China began with the Shang dynasty. Elaborate containers like this were used in religious ceremonies.

c.1500-600 Vedic Period in
India. Religious poems called the
Vedas are composed, and passed on by
word of mouth. They become the
basis for the Hindu religion. The
Aryans set up several kingdoms, each
ruled by a *rajah*, and divide people
into social classes: priests, warriors,
farmers, traders and Dravidians
(non-Aryans). This is the
origin of the Hindu
caste system.

c.1400 First
examples of
writing in
China.

Chinese writing on an oracle bone; a bone that was thought to show messages about the future.

c.1027-221 Zhou dynasty overthrows
the Shang in China. Period of trade
and economic growth, but also of
instability and wars.

Ornament for a horse's chariot, found in a grave near Loyang, the Zhou capital.

The Americas

c.2000BC People settle in the Arctic.

c.2000 First evidence of farmers
growing corn and metal-working in
Peru.

c.2000-1500 Pottery spreads among
farmers in Peru.

c.2000-1000 The beginning of Mayan
culture in Mesoamerica (Central
America). This is known as the Early
Pre-Classical Period. Farmers begin to
settle in villages.

c.1800-900 The Initial Period in Peru.
People settle in permanent villages,
and there is evidence of social and
religious organization. The use of
pottery spreads.

c.1500 North America: agriculture
reaches the southeast and, rather later,
the midwest.

c.1500BC-AD200 Rise of the Olmec
culture on the coast of the Gulf of
Mexico. The Olmecs use hieroglyphics
(picture writing) and
calendars. They
build ceremonial
architecture at
La Venta and
other sites,
and carve
huge heads
from a stone
called basalt
and small jade
figures.

This huge head was carved from a single block of stone.

c.1200 A series of
temples is built at
San Lorenzo,
Mexico, by the Olmec people.

c.1200-300 Chavín people create the
first civilization in South America.
Skilled stoneworkers, they build huge
temples filled with sculptures and are
the first people in South America to
make things from gold.

This gold ornament may have been made for a Chavín priest.

Europe

c.900BC The Etruscans are established in northern Italy. They are skilled at working in metal.

c.800 Greek poet Homer composes the *Iliad* and the *Odyssey*: epic poems describing the Trojan Wars.

Etruscans made many statues of warriors like this one.

c.800 First evidence of a Celtic culture in Hallstatt (Austria).

THE FOUNDING OF ROME

From about **1000BC**, groups of Indo-Europeans, skilled in working in iron, settled in Italy. One group, the Latins, built villages on the edge of the Tiber river, which grew to become the city of Rome. Traditionally founded in **753BC**, Rome became the focus of a great civilization which lasted nearly 1000 years. The early Romans were ruled by kings until **510-509BC**, when a republic was set up.

776 Traditional date for the first Olympic Games in Greece.

c.750 Greek city-states begin to found colonies in Turkey.

c.700-500 Bronze Age culture named after Hallstatt in Austria, with evidence of salt-mining and iron-working.

URNFIELD CULTURE

HALLSTATT CULTURE • Hallstatt

SCYTHIANS

Thracians

Hittites

Greeks

c.700 Indo-European people called the Scythians spread from central Asia to eastern Europe. They raid nearby lands from **c.700-600BC**.

683 Athens replaces its hereditary kings with nine archons (chief magistrates), chosen yearly by the nobles.

c.600-500 The Archaic Period in Greek art.

594 Solon is made sole archon of Athens. He introduces government reforms.

514 Scythians fight off an attack by Persians.

Scythian horseman

510 Roman republic is established. It is ruled by the Senate, a group of 100 men, called senators, from leading families.

c.508 Greek politician Cleisthenes introduces reforms which lead to democracy in Athens.

The Middle East

c.1000BC The Arabs tame camels.

c.965-928 Solomon rules Israel. Temple built at Jerusalem.

c.926 Israel splits into Israel and Judah.

THE NEW ASSYRIAN EMPIRE

The New Assyrian empire lasted from **c.911-609BC**. At its peak, it covered Mesopotamia and mountains to the east, Syria, Lebanon, Palestine and Lower Egypt. The Assyrians built great cities with palaces and temples.

Ashurnasirpal II (883–859BC)

874 First evidence of Nabataean people in Arabia.

835-825 Kingdom of Urartu (or Ararat) around Lake Van, Turkey, major base for iron and copper trade. Conquered by Assyrians (**721-715**), then Scythians and Medes (**610**).

c.800 Kingdom of Phrygia is established.

c.730 Babylon becomes part of the Assyrian empire.

722-705 Reign of Sargon II of Assyria. Height of Assyria's military power. He conquers Israel and sacks Babylon.

704-681 Reign of Sennacherib of Assyria. He conquers Phoenicia (**701**) and builds a new capital at Nineveh.

c.700-546 Kingdom of Lydia. First to develop coins.

c.700-600 Kingdoms of Persia and Media are set up.

689 Babylon is destroyed by the Assyrians.

668-627 Reign of Ashurbanipal of Assyria.

625-605 Reign of Nabopolassar, who becomes King of Babylon, setting up the New Babylonian empire.

612-609 Assyrian empire collapses.

605-561 Reign of Nebuchadnezzar II. Rebuilds Babylon, making it a great city. Destroys Jerusalem in **587**.

560-546 Croesus of Lydia takes control of most Greek colonies in Asia Minor (Turkey).

559-530 Cyrus II rules Persia. Conquers Assyria in **550**, Lydia and cities in Turkey in **546** and Babylon in **539**.

The Ishtar Gate, Babylon

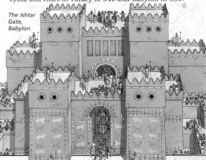

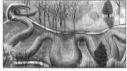

1000BC

Africa

814BC Founding of Carthage in North Africa by the Phoenician princess, Elissa of Tyre.

750-664 Egypt is ruled by kings from Kush (dynasty XXV), who are later driven back south, where they set up the kingdom of Meroë.

King Taharka of Kush (690–664BC)

A pyramid at Meroë

c.700 Cattle and sheep are domesticated in West Africa.

671 Assyrians conquer Egypt.

664-332 Late Period in Egypt, dynasties XXVI-XXX. Egypt is reunited by princes from Sais.

663 The use of iron tools and weapons spreads in North Africa.

c.650 Carthage builds up her fleet to protect colonies in the Mediterranean.

c.590 Meroë becomes the capital city of Kush.

Sahara rock painting of herdsmen with their cattle

525-404 Persia conquers and rules most of Egypt.

510 First of several treaties between Carthage and Rome, ensuring Carthage's trade monopoly in the western Mediterranean.

Asia

c.800BC Hindu religion spreads into southern India.

Hindu symbol known as the "wheel of life", representing the cycle of life, death and rebirth

660 Legendary date for the founding of Japan under Emperor Jimmu. In fact, Japan was probably not united under a monarchy until c.120.

c.650 Iron-working begins in China.

c.600 Probable date for the introduction of the religion and philosophy of Taoism, by the Chinese philosopher Lao-tze.

Taoist symbol representing the harmony between the two opposing forces of the universe, known as yin (female) and yang (male)

c.560-480 Life of Gautama Siddhartha, known as the Buddha, Indian founder of Buddhist religion.

Head of the Buddha from Gandhara, India

c.551-479 Life of Kung Fu-tze, also known as Confucius, Chinese philosopher. He lived in a time of warfare and believed peace could only be restored if people followed a strict code of conduct.

Confucius

512 Indian provinces of Sind and Gandhara become part of Persian empire.

The Americas

c.1000-300BC The Adena people are based around the Ohio River Valley in North America. They live in small groups, farming corn and beans. They also construct burial mounds and earthworks for ceremonial buildings.

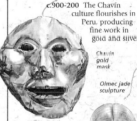

Snake-shaped Adena burial mound

c.900 Mexico: San Lorenzo is destroyed. Olmecs build the first ball court at La Venta, for use in religious festivals, rather than sport.

c.900-200 The Chavín culture flourishes in Peru, producing fine work in gold and silver.

Chavín gold mask

Olmec jade sculpture

c.700 Founding of Monte Albán, sacred city of the Olmecs, in Oaxaca, Mexico.

c.600 Oaxaca becomes the base for Olmec culture.

CENTRAL AMERICA   Gulf of Mexico

Teotihuacán   El Tajín

Monte Albán   La Venta   OLMECS   Tikal

OAXACA   MAYA

Map showing early Central American cultures

501BC

Europe

CLASSICAL GREECE

The period from **c.500-338BC** in Greece is known as the Classical Period. It was the great age of the Greek city-states. Ideas of art, architecture, literature, drama, politics, philosophy, science and history developed at this time provided the foundations for European civilization. Much of the activity was based in Athens, where commerce, as well as culture, thrived. Rivalry between the cities, and between Athens and Sparta in particular, led ultimately to the Peloponnesian Wars, which tore the Greek world apart and ended the Classical Period.

A reconstruction of the Parthenon temple in Athens, built between c.447-438BC.

500-494BC Greek colonists in Turkey rebel against Persians.

490 and 480-479 Wars between Persia and Greece.

490 Greeks defeat Persians at Battle of Marathon.

479 Greeks defeat Persians at Battle of Plataea.

461-429 Pericles is active in Athenian politics.

c.450 Celtic culture, named after a site at La Tène in France.

431-404 The Peloponnesian Wars in Greece.

c.390 Rome is sacked by the Gauls, a Celtic tribe.

359-336 Reign of Philip II of Macedon, in northern Greece.

338 Philip II defeats Greek cities at Chaeronea.

ALEXANDER THE GREAT

Alexander (**336-323BC**) came to power after the murder of his father, Philip of Macedon. A brilliant military commander, he extended his empire as far as India, earning the title Alexander the Great. After his death in **323BC**, at the age of 33, his generals, the Diadochi, fought for control of his empire. **By 281BC**, it had split into three kingdoms, ruled by the descendants of three Diadochi: Ptolemy, Antigonas and Seleucus. Although his empire did not last, it spread Greek language and culture over a wide area. The period 323-30BC is often described as the Hellenistic Age, after *Hellene*, meaning Greek.

Mosaic of Alexander defeating the Persians at the Battle of Issus, 333

280-168 Antigonid dynasty rules Macedonia.

279 Celts attack and rob the Greek temple at Delphi.

264-241 1st Punic War between Carthage and Rome.

The Middle East

THE PERSIAN EMPIRE

The Persians first arrived in the area now called Iran in **c.700BC**. King Cyrus II (**559-530BC**) united Persia with the rival kingdom of Media in 550BC and expanded his territory, taking over Lydia, Greek cities in Asia Minor and Babylon. The empire was at its height under Darius I (**522-486**), who made Persia the largest empire the world had ever seen. He also established a fair and efficient administrative and legal system, and built roads linking Persia with its far-flung provinces.

Persian armlet made of solid gold

This painting of one of the Persian elite warriors, known as the Immortals, is taken from the palace at Susa, Persia.

c.500BC-AD100 Kingdom of Sabaea on the south coast of Arabia is at its most powerful.

486-465 Xerxes I rules Persia.

4th century BC Nabataeans build a city in rock at Petra, Jordan. They dominate rich trade in goods as far as India.

332 Alexander conquers Phoenicia.

331-330 Alexander conquers Persia. Persepolis is burned.

304-64 Seleucid empire controls Asia Minor, Mesopotamia, Persia and India, but is gradually reduced in size.

c.280-47 Kingdom of Pontus, founded by Mithridates I.

279 Celts set up kingdom of Galatia in Turkey.

279-74 Kingdom of Bithynia established.

Ruins of the city of Petra, in the Nabataean kingdom

263-133 Kingdom of Pergamum, founded by Eumenes I.

247BC-AD277 Kingdom of Parthia established.

Africa

c.500BC-AD400 Nubian kings move their capital south to Meroë. A new phase of cultural development follows, with the building of towns, temples, palaces and pyramids, all showing Egyptian influence.

c.500BC-AD200 Nok civilization in Nigeria.

Nok sculptors made life size pottery heads.

c.500BC-AD500 Bantu people move through Africa.

343-332 Egypt is conquered and occupied by Persia.

332 Egypt is conquered by Alexander the Great.

323-30 The Ptolemaic dynasty (descended from Ptolemy, one of Alexander's generals) rules Egypt from Alexandria. It becomes an important base for learning, invention, and the largest city in the Greek world.

Alexandria lighthouse, one of the wonders of the ancient world

Asia

500BC-AD300 Yayoi culture in Japan is influenced by people who come from China and Korea with bronze making skills. Rice farming and metalwork begin.

481-221 The Warring States Period in China: all seven kingdoms of China are at war with each other.

327-325 Alexander the Great campaigns in India.

321-185 The first Indian empire is founded in northern India by Chandragupta Maurya, who begins the Maurya dynasty in India. He seizes the kingdom of Magadha and then takes control of much of Pakistan and Afghanistan.

Indian war elephants

272-231 India: reign of King Asoka of the Maurya dynasty. He unites northern and central India and builds a network of roads. Despite his early reputation as a warrior, he later becomes a Buddhist and abandons military conquests.

Capital of a column erected by Indian King Asoka

The Americas

c.500BC-AD200 The Paracas culture in southern Peru. The people are skilled at weaving and embroidery.

Paracas embroidery

c.400BC Mexico: Olmec city of La Venta is abandoned.

c.300 Gradual decline of the Olmec culture in Mexico. Rise of Zapotec culture in Oaxaca region.

c.300BC-250AD Rise of the Maya in Central America the Late Pre Classical Period. Important political and religious bases develop around stone cities such as Monte Albán, Teotihuacán and El Tajín.

Mayan mask

Part of a Mayan calendar. Dots, dashes and curved lines indicate dates.

c.300BC-550AD North America: the Hopewell people displace the Adenas. They are great mound-builders and traders.

Europe

218-201BC 2nd Punic War between the Carthaginians, from North Africa, and the Romans: Hannibal of Carthage crossed the Alps into Italy, with an army that included 40 war elephants.

Hannibal's army crossing the Alps with his war elephants

215-205, 200-197 and **171-163** Wars between Rome and Macedonia end in the partition of Macedonia.

149-146 3rd Punic war between Rome and Carthage ends in Roman victory. Carthage is destroyed.

146 Greece becomes part of the Roman empire.

110-106 Scythian lands are conquered by King Mithrides of Pontus, on the Black Sea.

102-101 General Marius defeats Germanic tribes invading the Roman empire.

82-79 Sulla becomes Roman dictator, followed by Pompey (52-46).

58-51 Julius Caesar, a Roman general, conquers Gaul (France).

45-44 Caesar is Roman dictator. He is assassinated and civil war follows.

31 Battle of Actium: Caesar's heir, Octavian, defeats Roman politician Mark Antony and Cleopatra, Queen of Egypt, and becomes ruler of Rome.

A Roman legionary (foot soldier)

The Middle East

247BC-AD277 Parthian kingdom is founded in Central Asia. Mithridates I (171-138BC) extends control in Persia and Mesopotamia.

168 Judas Maccabeus leads Jews against the Seleucids.

133 The last king of Pergamum in Asia Minor bequeathes his kingdom to Rome.

c.100BC-AD150 Nabataea (Jordan) is rich and powerful.

88-64 Kingdom of Pontus is gradually reduced in size after war with Rome.

74 Kingdom of Bithynia passes under Roman rule.

64 Palestine becomes the Roman province of Judea.

Map of the Hellenistic world c.200BC

47 Battle of Zela: Julius Caesar conquers the kingdom of Pontus.

37-4 Rule of Herod the Great, King of Judea.

c.5 Birth of Jesus Christ in Bethlehem, Judea.

Jesus's mother Mary on her way to Bethlehem

THE ROMAN EMPIRE

Emperor Augustus

In 27BC, Octavian became the first Roman emperor, taking the title Augustus, and ruling until **AD14**. The empire lasted about 500 years. It expanded across the whole of the Mediterranean, reaching its greatest extent under emperors Trajan (**AD98-117**) and Hadrian (**AD117-138**). But from **c.AD200** its borders were frequently under attack by barbarian tribes and the empire was beset by other problems: economic recession, civil wars and a succession of weak or corrupt emperors. In **AD476**, the empire finally came to an end.

Map of Roman empire, showing movements of barbarian tribes

Vandals, Alans, Suevi / Jutes, Angles, Saxons / Franks / Goths / Visigoths / Ostrogoths / Alemanni / Lombards / Burgundians

250BC

1BC

Africa

203BC The Romans defeat the Carthaginians at Tunis, North Africa.

202 The Romans destroy the Carthaginian army at Zama, Tunisia.

146 Carthage is destroyed and becomes a Roman province.

Roman legionaries, the well-trained soldiers who conquered a huge empire

111-105 Jugurtha of Numidia, in North Africa, is defeated by the Roman general Marius, and his kingdom is absorbed by Rome.

30 Egypt becomes a Roman province after Queen Cleopatra is defeated by the Roman leader Octavian.

Queen Cleopatra VII, shown in this Egyptian style portrait, was the last of the Greek Ptolemy dynasty to rule Egypt.

Asia

THE QIN DYNASTY

In 221BC, the Qin (or Ch'in) kingdom conquered the six other kingdoms of China and the Qin ruler named himself Shi Huangdi, or "first emperor of China". In 214BC, he built the Great Wall of China, a 3460km (2150 mile) wall to protect China from invaders called Hsiung-Nu (Huns). When the emperor died in 210BC, he was placed in a vast tomb, watched over by an army of terracotta (pottery) model soldiers.

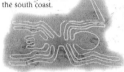

The Great Wall of China

c.200BC Three kingdoms in South India.

c.200 India is invaded by Bactrians and Parthians. Small Greek states are set up in the Punjab from c.170.

THE HAN DYNASTY

There was unrest in China after the death of Shi Huangdi. Then, in 202BC, the Han dynasty took control, when a soldier named Liu Bang made himself emperor. His dynasty ruled until AD220, and China grew in size and prosperity.

Chinese nobleman

c.185 India: end of Mauryan empire.

c.150BC-AD50 Bronze age culture in North Vietnam, named after the village of Dong-son.

140-87 China expands under Emperor Wuti to include Korea and North Vietnam. He develops an efficient civil service, reduces the power of the nobles, and builds a network of roads and canals.

c.100s North India is invaded by Greeks and nomadic tribes.

The Americas

c.200BC-AD200 Paracas Necropolis culture flourishes in Peru. Brilliant embroidered textiles have been found in a cemetery from this period.

c.200BC-AD600 Peru: regional development and technological experiments among the Moche people of the north coast and the Nazca people of the south coast.

This 45m (148ft) long giant spider was carved in the desert by the Nazca people.

c.200BC-AD700 The rise of the culture of Teotihuacán in Mexico.

c.100BC North America: Hohokam people in the southeast build ditches and dykes to irrigate their crops. They also build platform mounds and ball courts.

Nazca pottery

South American vegetables

Squash

Potatoes

Pepper

Chilli peppers

Europe

AD43 Romans conquer Britain.

61 Queen Boudicca of the Iceni, a British tribe, leads a revolt against the Romans in East Anglia.

The Arch of Titus, commemorating the capture of Jerusalem by Rome in AD70

72-80 The Colosseum is built in Rome.

79 The volcano Vesuvius erupts in Italy.

98-117 Reign of Emperor Trajan: the Roman empire reaches its greatest extent.

122-127 Hadrian's Wall is built to mark the northern frontier of the Roman empire in Britain.

c.200 Germanic tribes attack the frontiers of the Roman empire.

286 Emperor Diocletian splits the Roman empire into East and West.

312 Constantine becomes emperor of the Western Roman empire.

Portrait of a Christian family in Roman times

313 Edict of Milan: Christians granted freedom to worship in Roman empire.

324-337 Constantine reunites the Roman empire.

c.370 Huns invade Europe from Central Asia.

378 Battle of Adrianople: Roman emperor Valens is killed by barbarian tribes called Goths.

391 Emperor Theodosius makes Christianity the state religion in the Roman empire.

395 Roman empire is permanently split into East and West.

401-413 Visigoths invade Italy and sack Rome. The Roman capital is moved to Ravenna, Italy.

c.410-520 Angles, Saxons and Jutes settle in England.

415 Visigoths found kingdom of Toulouse.

443-534 Burgundian kingdom in Rhône-Saône area, France.

451 Battle of Châlons, France: Romans and Franks halt the invasions of Huns in Europe.

455 Barbarian tribes of Vandals sack Rome.

456-711 Visigoth kingdom established in Spain.

457 Anglo-Saxons establish seven kingdoms in Britain.

476 Rome is sacked: the end of the Western Roman empire.

481-511 Reign of Clovis, King of the Franks. Founds the Merovingian dynasty. He becomes a Christian in 496.

493 Italian kingdom of Theodoric of the Ostrogoths.

The Middle East

AD26-36 Pontius Pilate is governor of Judea.

c.29 Jesus Christ is crucified.

45-48, 49-52, 54-58 Paul of Tarsus makes missionary journeys around the eastern Mediterranean, spreading Christianity. He travels to Rome in 58-60.

66-73 Jewish revolt against the Romans in Judea. The Romans sack Jerusalem in 70 and destroy the Jewish stronghold of Masada in 73.

106 The Nabataean kingdom becomes a Roman province.

115-117 Jewish uprisings in Egypt, Cyrenaica and Cyprus.

131-135 Unsuccessful Jewish revolt, led by Bar Cochba. Jerusalem is destroyed.

Paul of Tarsus

227 The Sassanid dynasty is established in Persia by Ardashir I.

260 Shapur I of Persia defeats the Romans and captures Emperor Valerian.

268-272 Queen Zenobia of Palmyra conquers Syria, Mesopotamia and parts of Egypt.

310-379 Reign of Shapur II of Persia.

324 Constantine rebuilds Byzantium, renames it Constantinople, and makes it the Roman capital.

Roman ruins at Palmyra in Syria

325 First Council of the Christian Church meets at Nicaea in Anatolia (Turkey).

484 The Persian empire is attacked by Huns and the emperor is killed.

The Huns were armed horsemen from Central Asia. They used stirrups, then unknown to people farther west.

499

Africa

AD44 Mauretania (Morocco) is conquered by Rome.

70 Christianity reaches Alexandria. Starts spreading south from c.180.

100-700 Civilization of Axum (Ethiopia): a trading state which derives its wealth from maritime trade and the export of ivory.

Areas where rock paintings have been found

Sandstone sculpture from Meroë

193-211 A Libyan, Septimius Severus, becomes Roman emperor.

238 Revolt begins in North Africa against Roman rule.

c.285 Monastic life starts in Egypt.

c.300-1200 Kingdom of Ghana.

c.330-350 King Ezana rules Axum.

c.333 The state of Axum converts to Christianity.

Obelisk from Axum

c.350 Axum conquers Meroë and becomes the dominant power in the Red Sea area.

c.350-600 The X-group culture flourishes in Nubia.

c.400 The first towns appear south of the Sahara Desert.

c.400 The use of iron spreads in East Africa.

429-533 Vandal kingdom is set up in North Africa.

Asia

AD1-100 Buddhism spreads from India throughout Asia.

8-25 Hsin dynasty in China.

25-222 Han dynasty is restored in China: a new age of Chinese culture.

c.50 Nomadic tribes from Bactria, Central Asia, establish the Kushan empire in northern India.

91 Chinese defeat the Huns in Mongolia.

c.100 Paper is invented in China.

c.100 Buddhism reaches China.

Flying horse bronze statue from Kansu, China

c.100-1600 The Champa kingdom is set up in Southeast Asia.

c.180 Tribes start to unite in Japan.

c.195-405 Parthians control northern India.

222-265 The Han dynasty in China is replaced by three separate states.

265-316 China is divided into many small states.

c.285 Traditional date for the introduction of writing to Japan.

c.300-500 Yamato government in Japan. Society is organized into clans, who follow the Shinto religion.

304 Huns break through the Great Wall in northern China.

316 Japan invades Korea.

316-589 Rival dynasties established in north and south China.

320-535 Gupta empire in India is founded by Chandragupta II. Classical Age in India.

Statue of the god Vishnu from the Gupta period

c.400 Settlers from Southeast Asia reach Easter Island.

430-470 Gupta empire breaks up after Huns invade.

c.450 Writing comes to Japan from China.

The Americas

c.AD1-500 Basket makers culture in the southwest of North America.

c.50 Central America: city of Teotihuacán is built, including the Great Pyramid of the Sun.

Pyramid of the Sun, Teotihuacán

c.200-600 Growth of civilization around the city of Tiahuanaco, near Lake Titicaca in Bolivia.

c.250-750 The Classical Period of the Zapotec culture in Mexico.

c.500 Central America: Teotihuacán is rich and powerful.

The powerful jaguar, native to South America

THE MAYA

One of the greatest early American civilizations was that of the Maya, which lasted from c.2000BC-AD1460. The Maya built cities deep in the Central American jungle, worshipped many gods and studied the stars. Mayan culture reached its peak in the Classical Period (c.AD250-900). They invented calendars, picture writing and number systems, and their astronomers developed advanced mathematical skills.

The Maya played a ball game as part of a religious ceremony.

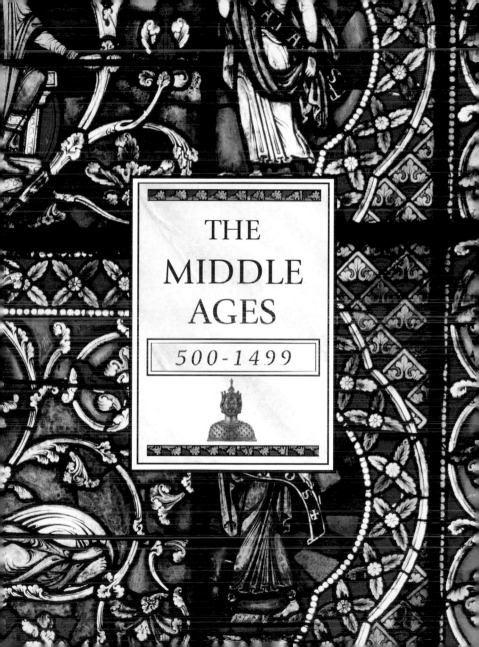

THE
MIDDLE
AGES

500-1499

Southern and Western Europe

c.500-843 Frankish kingdom in France and Germany.

507-711 Visigoth kingdom in Spain.

Visigoth crown belonging to King Recceswinth

529 St. Benedict founds the first monastery in Western Europe, at Monte Cassino, Italy.

c.537 Death of King Arthur of the Britons, at the Battle of Camlan.

Arthur, famous for his Knights of the Round Table, is shown here as a knight. He may have been a British chief who fought the invading Saxons.

553 Emperor Justinian takes control of Ostrogoth kingdom in northern Italy.

554 Emperor Justinian conquers part of the Visigoth kingdom in Spain.

563 St.Columba, an Irish monk, founds a monastery on Iona, and sends missionaries to England and Scotland.

568-774 Lombard kingdom in northern Italy.

596 St. Augustine is sent to Britain by Pope Gregory to convert the Saxons to Christianity.

Augustine preaching

c.600 England is divided into seven kingdoms.

664 Synod of Whitby: English Christians choose Roman rather than Celtic (Irish) branch of Christianity.

c.695 Lindisfarne Gospels are produced: the first book of psalms in Anglo-Saxon.

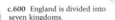

An Anglo-Saxon helmet found in a ship grave in East Anglia

Northern and Eastern Europe

c.500-700 Slavs begin migrating from the Pripet region, west of the Dnieper river, to the forest areas of Russia and Eastern Europe.

JUSTINIAN AND THE BYZANTINE EMPIRE

The eastern Roman empire, usually known as the Byzantine empire, survived for a thousand years after the fall of Rome. Based in Constantinople (originally Byzantium, and now Istanbul), it was a major political power and helped to preserve classical learning and Christianity through the Eastern (Orthodox) Church.One of the greatest

Mosaic from Ravenna of Justinian's empress, Theodora

Byzantine emperors was Justinian (527-565). He rebuilt much of the city and organized the legal system into the Justinian code (528-534), the basis for modern European law. He also struggled to reconquer the old Roman empire, taking control of the Vandal kingdom in North Africa in 535, the Ostrogoth kingdom in Italy in 553, and part of the Spanish Visigoth kingdom in 554. But these reconquests were lost after his death.

540-561 War between Persia and the Byzantine empire.

568 Lombards take northern Italy from the Byzantines.

c.600 Avars, a nomadic people from the Steppes of Central Asia, establish a kingdom in the Balkans.

603-629 Wars between Persia and the Byzantine empire.

610-641 Reign of Byzantine Emperor Heraclius. The official language changes from Latin to Greek.

611-616 Byzantines lose territory in the Middle East, North Africa, Spain and Sicily to the Persians.

629 Emperor Heraclius wins back territory from Persia

632-750 Arabs attack the Byzantine empire.

674-678 Arabs unsuccessfully besiege Constantinople.

c.680 Bulgars, a nomadic people from Central Asia, invade the Balkans and establish a Bulgar state.

Church of St. Sophia, Constantinople, built in Justinian's reign

Africa and the Middle East

531 Justinian sends a group of monks, led by Julian, to the Christian kingdom of Axum, Ethiopia.

531-579 Chrosroes I rules the Persian Sassanid empire. The empire is at its greatest extent.

533-697 Byzantines rule North Africa.

543 Julian spreads Christianity to Nubia, which is divided into three Christian kingdoms - Nobatia, Makuria and Alodia. They are cut off from the rest of Christendom by the Arab conquest of Egypt (see below).

MOHAMMED AND THE RISE OF ISLAM

The prophet Mohammed (c.570-632), founder of Islam, was born in Mecca, Arabia. In 610, he began preaching that there was only one God, Allah, and won many converts. After local hostility, he was forced to flee to Medina (622), where he organized his followers. By his death, Islam had spread throughout most of Arabia - by means of conquest and conversion. He was succeeded by a series of elected caliphs, who created a vast Islamic empire between 632-850.

A mosque, a Muslim place of worship

611-619 Persians conquer Byzantine territory in Middle East and North Africa: Antioch, Damascus, Jerusalem and Egypt.

632 Mohammed is succeeded by Abu Bakr, who becomes first caliph.

637-638 Arabs overrun Syria and Iraq and Jerusalem.

639-642 Arabs occupy Egypt.

642 Arabs overthrow Sassanids. Persia adopts Shi'ite branch of Islam.

661-750 Omayyad dynasty rules from Damascus.

697-700 Arabs conquer Carthage and Tunis. North African coast converts to Islam.

The Great Mosque at Kairouan, North Africa

Asia

c.500 Yamato emperors control most of Japan.

535 Gupta empire collapses. India divides into warring kingdoms.

552 Buddhism is introduced into Japan from China.

581 General Yang Chien founds the Sui dynasty. He unites China in 589.

594 Buddhism becomes the Japanese state religion.

605-610 China: millions of people are drafted to build the Imperial Canal, linking the rivers Yangtze and Huang Ho.

606 Written examinations are introduced in China for entry into the civil service.

607 Tibet is politically unified.

618-907 T'ang dynasty in China: one of China's most brilliant periods, in terms of the arts and military conquest.

624 Buddhism becomes the official religion in China.

627-649 Reign of T'ai tsung the Great, Emperor of China.

Emperor T'ai tsung

c.628-645 Hsuan-tsang travels from China to northern India, returning home with manuscripts and statues.

645 Buddhism reaches Tibet.

657 Chinese defeat Turks and extend their power in Central Asia.

668 Chinese take Pyongyang, capital of Korea.

690-713 Empress Wu siezes the throne in China.

The Americas

c.500 North America: Hopewellian mound-builders begin to decline. Mississippi mound-builders start to appear at the lower end of the Mississippi River.

Pottery bottles made by Mississippi mound-builders

c.500-900 Golden age of the Zapotec culture in Oaxaca, Mexico.

c.500-1700 Culture of the central Gulf coast of Mexico, also known as Totonac, based around El Tajín.

c.600 Peak of Mayan civilization.

A Mayan king with his servant

c.600 The Teotihuacán culture is at its peak, extending from the city to surrounding highlands. The city is about 20km (8 miles) square and laid out on a grid. Its wealth comes from agriculture, crafts and trade.

A later Mexican city, Tenochtitlán, built c.1325

c.600-1000 The Middle Horizon Period in South America. Large towns are built. Local cultures are merged under two great empires, based around Tiahuanaco, an important religious base, and Huari, a military capital.

c.650-850 Teotihuacán culture slowly declines.

c.650-900 Huastecan culture in Mexico.

Southern and Western Europe

c.700s Great age of art and literature in Ireland.

711 North African Arabs, known as "Moors", conquer Spain, except the northwestern kingdom of Asturias.

732 Battle of Poitiers: Arabs advance into France and are defeated by Frankish leader Charles Martel and forced to retreat.

756-1031 Arab Omayyad caliphate rules from Córdoba, southern Spain.

751 Pepin III deposes the last Merovingian king of France and becomes first Carolingian king of France.

The Ardagh cup, looted by Vikings in Ireland

CHARLEMAGNE

In **768**, the kingdom of Pepin III was inherited by his sons, Carloman and Charles. When Carloman died in **771**, Charles became sole ruler (**771-814**). A brilliant soldier, he built up the Frankish empire between **773-804** to include most of France, Germany and northern Italy, earning the title Charlemagne ("Charles the Great"). A committed Christian, he campaigned against non-Christian kingdoms and built churches and monasteries all over his empire. In **800**, the Pope crowned him "Emperor of the Romans" in recognition of this.

A golden bust of Charlemagne decorated with precious stones

751 Lombards conquer Ravenna, the last Byzantine possession in north Italy.

757-796 Reign of Offa of Mercia. Builds a dyke to keep out the Welsh. Becomes ruler of all England by **779**.

c.790-794 Vikings begin raiding Europe. They plunder Lindisfarne and Jarrow, England.

806 Vikings raid a monastery on Iona, a Scottish island. Monks flee to Ireland.

c.830-900 Frequent Viking raids on the British Isles and France.

832-847 Vikings raid and settle in Ireland.

843 Kenneth MacAlpin, King of the Scots tribe, becomes King of Scotland.

843 Charlemagne's empire is split into three kingdoms.

858 Rhodri Mawr is recognized as Prince of all Wales.

867-874 Danes conquer Mercia, Northumbria and East Anglia.

871-899 Reign of Alfred the Great of Wessex. He resists further conquests by the Danes. England is divided into Wessex and the Danelaw.

Alfred fighting a Dane

Northern and Eastern Europe

THE VIKINGS

The Vikings were farmers, traders and warriors from Scandinavia. Increasing population and shortage of land at home drove some to raiding and looting. Between **c.800-1100**, they terrorized much of Europe. But the Vikings were also skilled shipbuilders and navigators, and they sailed as far as North America in search of new land. Many settled peacefully in Normandy in France (named after "Northmen") and Russia, where they founded the first Russian state, named after a Viking tribe, the Rus.

c.700 Vikings first arrive in Russia.

716-1018 Bulgar state recognized by the Byzantine emperor.

716-717 Arabs unsuccessfully besiege Constantinople.

717 Byzantines ally with Bulgars and Khazars.

726-843 Iconoclasm: Byzantine emperors prohibit the use of icons (religious pictures) and many are destroyed.

787 Church Council of Nicaea orders the restoration of icons in churches.

812 Battle of Adrianople: Khan Krum of Bulgaria defeats the Byzantines and kills their emperor.

830 Slav kingdom of Moravia is established. It is destroyed by Magyars in **906**.

c.860 Swedish Vikings settle in Russia.

861 Vikings discover Iceland and settle there in **874**.

862 St. Cyril and St. Methodius work as Christian missionaries in Moravia. Cyril adapts the Greek alphabet for the Slavs. It becomes known as the Cyrillic alphabet.

Mosaic of Jesus Christ, from St. Sophia, Constantinople

c.862 Rurik of the Rus tribe of Vikings founds a Russian state, based in Novgorod.

866 Conversion of Russia to Christianity begins.

867-1056 Macedonian dynasty rules Byzantine empire.

882 Russian ruler Oleg the Wise conquers Kiev.

889 Magyars invade Hungary and set up a state under the Arpad dynasty (**896-1301**).

c.890s-930s Norway is first organized as a single kingdom, under Harald Fairhair.

700

899

Africa and the Middle East

c.700s Arab merchants develop a flourishing trade with rich Saharan trading cities. The Arabs bring horses, copper, tools and weapons in exchange for gold, ivory, skins and slaves. This encourages the growth of strong African kingdoms and trading empires.

African king receiving Arab traders in Timbuktu

c.700-1200 Kingdom of Ghana: the first West African trading empire, rich in gold.

750-1258 The Abbasid dynasty rules from Baghdad, Iraq: a golden age of Islamic culture.

Arab astronomers from the Abbasid period, taken from an Islamic illustration

786-809 Reign of Abbasid caliph Harun al Rashid, known for the *Thousand and One Nights* stories.

788 Shi'ite kingdom founded in Morocco.

c.800 Three small, independent Arab kingdoms are set up in North Africa.

c.800-1000 Kingdom of Igbo Ukwu in West Africa.

c.800-1800 Kingdom of Kanem-Bornu, a great trading empire in West Africa.

868-905 Tulunid dynasty rules Egypt and Syria.

Asia

c.700-900 The Sailendra kingdom in Southeast Asia.

c.700-1300 The Srivijaya kingdom in Southeast Asia.

710-794 First permanent Japanese capital city is established at Nara.

711 Arabs invade northern India.

745-840 Uighur empire established in Mongolia.

c.750-1000 Maoris from Pacific Polynesian islands reach New Zealand.

c.750 Three empires in India wage war against each other: Rajputana (northwest), Rashtrakuta (south), and Bengal (northeast). Arabs begin invading the Indus region.

751 Abbasids defeat Chinese armies at Talas River, ending China's influence in Central Asia.

794-1185 Heian Period in Japan: the emperor rules from Heian (now Kyoto). Power is increasingly in the hands of the nobles.

A Heian lute, inlaid with mother of pearl

Phoenix Hall, Heian, Japan

c.800-1400 Khmer dynasty established kingdom in Cambodia, Southeast Asia, based at Angkor.

842 Tibetan kingdom disintegrates.

c.858-1160 Fujiwara clan controls the government in Japan.

868 Earliest printed book, Buddhist *Diamond Sutra*, is produced in China.

886-1267 Chola kings control most of southern India.

The Americas

MISSISSIPPI VALLEY CULTURE

From c.700s, the farmers of the Mississippi Valley began to build towns. In the middle of the towns were flat-topped mounds, on which they built temples or houses for the chief. The biggest town, Cahokia, had over a hundred mounds.

Mississippi town showing flat top mounds

c.700-1000 North America: Hohokam farming communities in the southwest (Arizona) reach their most prosperous stage. They build platform mounds and play ball games, suggesting links with the Mayan people of Mexico.

Map of North and Central America c.700

- Iroquois
- Cahokia
- Mississippi and woodland farmers
- Anasazi
- Hohokam
- Maya

Map of North and Central America c.700

c.700-1000 Anasazi farmers emerge in southwestern North America.

c.750 Desert tribes in southwest of North America begin building villages, known as pueblos, with rooms stacked one above the other.

c.750 Central America: the city of Teotihuacán is destroyed.

c.750 Mayan civilization begins to decline.

c.850 Mayan civilization collapses. Many cities abandoned.

Southern and Western Europe

c.900-911 Vikings settle in Normandy.

910 Benedictine Abbey is founded at Cluny in Burgundy.

911 Rollo, a Viking chief, is made Duke of Normandy. He is given Rouen and surrounding land by the Frankish king, Charles the Simple, on condition that he swears allegiance, and becomes a Christian. The land is known as *terra Normannorum* ("the land of the northmen" in Latin).

Rollo being welcomed by the Archbishop of Rouen

912-961 Reign of Abd al-Rahman, Caliph of Córdoba in Spain: a period of prosperity and a flourishing of Arab culture.

917-921 King Edward of Wessex conquers the southern half of the Danelaw (Danish-occupied part of Britain).

924-939 Anglo-Saxon King Athelstan rules in England.

926 Athelstan seizes the Danelaw.

937 Athelstan repels an invasion by Vikings, Scots and Britons at the Battle of Brunanburh.

979-1013 Reign of Anglo-Saxon King Ethelred the Unready.

986-987 Reign of Louis V, last Carolingian king of France.

987-996 Hugh Capet becomes first king of the French Capetian dynasty. The dynasty rules France until **1328**.

991 Danes defeat the English at the Battle of Malden. The English are forced to pay Danegeld, a tax to prevent more Danish attacks.

A Viking longboat

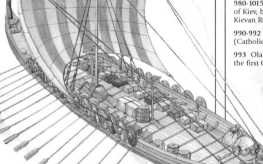

Northern and Eastern Europe

911 Death of Louis III ("the child"), last Carolingian king of Germany. Conrad of Franconia becomes King of Germany.

919-936 Reign of Henry I "the Fowler" of Saxony, first king of the Saxon dynasty in Germany.

929-967 Bohemia is united under Boleslav I, after he murders his brother Wenceslas.

933 Henry I of Germany defeats the Magyars.

Battle of Lechfeld

936-973 Reign of Otto I of Germany. He controls the German duchies and conquers Italy.

955 Battle of Lechfeld: Otto I stops the westward advance of the Magyars, a nomadic people from Central Asia.

960 Mieszko I (960-992) unites northern Poland and founds a Polish state.

961 Byzantines take Crete from the Arabs.

962 Otto I is crowned "Holy Roman Emperor of the German nation" and rules until 973.

965 Harald Bluetooth, King of Denmark, becomes a Christian.

Harald Bluetooth's rune stone, the Jelling Stone, showing an image of Jesus Christ

965 Russia destroys the Khazar empire.

970-997 Geza I controls the Magyars and unites Hungary.

976-1025 Reign of Basil II, Byzantine emperor. He wins victories against Arabs, Russians, Bulgarians, Armenians and Normans, and extends the Byzantine empire.

980-1015 Vladimir, Grand Prince of Kiev, becomes sole ruler of Kievan Russia.

990-992 Poland adopts the Western (Catholic) Church.

Vladimir of Kiev

993 Olaf Skötkonung becomes the first Christian king of Sweden.

995-1000 Reign of Olaf Tryggvason of Norway. Christianity is introduced.

997-1038 Reign of Stephen I (St. Stephen), first Christian king of Hungary.

Crown of Stephen I

Africa and the Middle East

c.900 West Africa: trade and prosperity grows in Hausaland, a region on the Lower Niger.

902-1004 The Samanid dynasty rules in Persia. With their capital at Bukhara in Samarkand, their empire covers the region between the Caspian Sea and the Hindu Kush mountains. They develop important trading contacts, both with China and the far north.

Samanid tomb at Bukhara, Central Asia

909-972 Fatimids take over the Arab kingdoms in North Africa.

Map of Fatimid caliphate

969-1171 Fatimids take control of Egypt. They build Cairo, which becomes the Egyptian capital.

c.970 Cairo University established.

997-1030 Reign of Mahmud, Sultan of Ghazni, who builds an empire in eastern Afghanistan and northern India. Ghazni becomes a base for Islamic culture.

Islamic city

Asia

c.900 The Mataram dynasty is established in Java, Indonesia.

907-960 Collapse of the T'ang dynasty in China is followed by the Epoch of the Five Dynasties. China is divided by civil wars.

916 Khitan kingdom is founded in Mongolia

936 Three kingdoms in Korea are united under the state of Koryo.

947-1125 Khitans overrun northern China and set up the Liao dynasty.

960-1127 Northern Sung dynasty reunites central and southern China and rules from Kaifeng.

985-1014 Reign of Rajara I, of the Chola kingdom, southern India. He conquers Kerala, South India (985) and Sri Lanka (1001).

Bronze statue of the Hindu god Shiva

990 Yangtu (Beijing) becomes the capital of northern China

The Americas

c.900 The heart of Mayan culture shifts to the Yucatán peninsula.

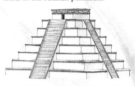

Pyramid of Quetzalcoatl at Chichén Itzá on the Yucatán peninsula, Mexico

c.900 Anasazi people, from southwest of North America, begin building pueblos, clusters of buildings nestling in cliffs, reached only by ladders. They weave cotton cloth, make pots using a wheel, and work in turquoise and other stones.

c.900-1200 Toltecs dominate much of Mexico. They destroy towns around Teotihuacán and invade Mayan territory.

Statue of a Toltec warrior

c.900-1494 Mixtec culture in Mexico.

947 Mexico: birth of Quetzalcoatl, revered by the Toltecs as a god.

980 The Toltecs establish a capital at Tula.

982 Eric the Red, a Viking, begins to colonize Greenland.

In Greenland, the Vikings came across Inuit people, like this man.

c.990s Quetzalcoatl flees from Tula after feuds between his followers and those of another man god. He settles in the Mayan city Chichén, which is renamed Chichén Itzá. The city is rebuilt in a mixture of Mayan and Toltec styles.

Southern and Western Europe

1004 Brian Boru is proclaimed "High King" of Ireland.

1008-1028 Moorish kingdom of Córdoba in Spain starts to weaken because of civil wars. Followed by the *reconquista*, the reconquest of the Muslim kingdoms of Spain and Portugal by the Christian Spanish kingdoms, which takes place between **1037-1492**.

The Great Mosque at Córdoba

1014-1042 Danish kings rule England.

1014 Brian Boru defeats the Vikings at Battle of Clontarf, but is killed in battle.

1016 Normans, led by Robert and Roger Guiscard, invade southern Italy.

1029 Spain: provinces of Castile and Aragon become independent of Moorish rule.

1042-1066 Reign of St. Edward the Confessor, King of England.

1054 Scotland: Macbeth, the Earl of Moray, is defeated and killed at Dunsinane by Malcolm Canmore, whose father, King Duncan, had been murdered by Macbeth.

1054 The Pope makes Robert Guiscard Duke of Apulia and Calabria and invites him to take Sicily from the Arabs.

1054 Eastern Orthodox Church splits from the Western Catholic Church.

1060-1130 Normans conquer Sicily and southern Italy. Roger Guiscard is made Count of Sicily (**1061-1091**).

1066 Battle of Hastings: William of Normandy conquers England, becoming King William I (**1066-1087**).

William of Normandy (left) and part of the Bayeux tapestry showing the Norman cavalry attacking English footsoldiers

1071 Normans conquer Bari, last Byzantine city in Italy.

1075-1122 Investiture Controversy: a quarrel between the Pope and the Holy Roman Emperor over who has the right to invest (or appoint) bishops and abbots. Settled at the Concordat of Worms (**1122**).

1085 Castile conquers Moorish province of Toledo. Hero of the struggle is Rodrigo Diaz de Vivar, known as El Cid.

1086 Domesday Book is compiled in England: a survey of all the property in the land.

1094 Portugal wins independence from Moorish Spain.

Northern and Eastern Europe

1001 Pope recognizes the Christian kingdom of Hungary.

1014-1035 Cnut, King of Denmark, rules an empire which covers Denmark, England and part of Sweden.

1015-1028 Reign of Olaf II ("the Saint"), King of Norway.

Above: Viking Christian symbols. In Cnut's reign, English missionaries converted the Danes to Christianity.

Left: map of Cnut's empire

A wooden church in Borgund, Norway

1019-1054 Yaroslav the Wise rules Kievan Russia.

1028 Cnut conquers Norway and Olaf flees to Russia.

1035 The kingdom of Norway is restored by Magnus the Good (**1035-1047**), after the death of Cnut.

1035 Poland becomes a fief (subject state) of the Holy Roman Empire.

1054 Schism (or split) between the Eastern Orthodox and Western Catholic Churches, after the Pope insists on supremacy over the whole Christian Church.

1059-1078 Dukas dynasty rules Byzantine empire.

1071 Battle of Manzikert: Byzantines are defeated by the Seljuk Turks and lose Asia Minor (Turkey).

1081-1085 Normans, led by Robert Guiscard, invade the Balkans.

Seljuk Turks, nomadic people from Central Asia

1081-1185 Comneni dynasty rules the Byzantine empire.

1086 Holy Roman Emperor recognizes Bohemia as a kingdom under Vratislav.

1093 Nomadic people called Polovtsy sack Russian capital, Kiev.

1095 Byzantine emperor, Alexius Comnenus (**1081-1118**), calls on Pope Urban II for help against the Turks.

c.1100 Viking raids end.

Africa and the Middle East

c.1000-1200 Trading ports grow up on the east coast of Africa.

c.1000-1450 Kingdom of Ife in West Africa.

c.1000-1897 Kingdom of Benin in West Africa.

c.1030 Seljuk Turks, nomadic people from Central Asia, extend their influence in Asia Minor.

c.1050-1123 Life of Omar Khayyam, Persian mathematician, astronomer and philosopher, and author of the *Rubaiyat*, a famous series of poems.

1052 Muslim Almoravids attack Ghana, which is destroyed by 1076.

1055 Seljuk Turks conquer Baghdad, the Abbasid capital.

1056-1147 Almoravid kingdom in North Africa and Spain.

1076 Seljuk Turks take Jerusalem and Damascus from the Fatimids. This provokes the Crusades.

THE CRUSADES

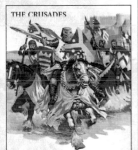

The Crusades were military expeditions fought by European Christians to win back the Holy Land (Palestine) from the Seljuk Turks. As militant Muslims, they were far less tolerant than the previous Fatimid rulers, and posed a real threat to Christian pilgrims. After the First Crusade (1096-1099), the crusaders took back Jerusalem and set up states in Anatolia and Syria, but these were later lost. There were seven further crusades, but with limited success. By 1291 the last Christian stronghold had disappeared.

c.1090 Assassins, a branch of Shi'ites who murder to destroy their opponents, are founded in Persia.

Asia

c.1000 Chinese perfect the invention of gunpowder.

Gunpowder was used in war and in firework displays.

c.1000 Maori people settle in New Zealand, after long sea voyages across the Pacific Ocean.

c.1000-1300 Kingdom of Pagan in Burma, Southeast Asia.

1001-1026 Mahmud of Ghazni leads raids on northern India and absorbs much of it into his empire.

1002-1050 Angkor kingdom in Cambodia grows in importance under King Suryavarman.

1020 Japan: *The Tale of Genji*, the first novel in any language, is written by Lady Murasaki Shikibu.

1051-1062 Nine Years' Civil War in Japan: the beginning of the rise of the samurai

THE SAMURAI

The samurai were a highly professional caste of warriors, who worked for Japanese feudal lords. They fought on horseback with bows and arrows, before closing in for hand-to-hand combat. Samurai were trained to win or die, and to give absolute loyalty to their lord, in return for gifts of land. They also helped to drive out foreign invaders. Running away from battle was seen as unforgivable, and samurai were sometimes even expected to commit ritual suicide, known as *seppuku*, or *harakiri*.

Samurai warrior

1083-1087 Three Years' Civil War in Japan.

The Americas

c.1000 Leif Ericsson, son of Eric the Red, travels along the North American coast, before returning to Greenland.

THE VIKINGS IN AMERICA

Viking explorers appear to have been the first Europeans to set foot in North America - almost 500 years before Christopher Columbus landed in the Caribbean. Leif Ericsson landed in three places on the East Coast which were probably Baffin Island, Labrador and Newfoundland. The remains of Viking-style buildings and other objects were dug up in Newfoundland in 1968.

Right: a statue of Leif Ericsson, in Iceland

Left: a Skraeling, the Viking name for Native Americans

c.1000 Hopewell people discover how to etch designs with acid.

c.1000 Northern Iroquois people settle around eastern Great Lakes and St. Lawrence River.

c.1000 Thule Eskimo people start to spread across the North American Arctic region.

c.1000-1483 Late Intermediate Period in South America. Decline of the Huari-Tiahuanaco culture. Local styles and cultures re-emerge.

Early Peruvian pot

c.1000-1600 The Easter Islanders, in the South Pacific, build huge stone heads.

Southern and Western Europe

1100

1105 Roger Guiscard II is Count of Sicily. He acquires Calabria (**1122**), Apulia (**1127**) and is made King of Sicily (**1130-1154**). The Normans rule Sicily until **1204**.

1128 Mathilda, heir to Henry I of England, marries Geoffrey of Anjou, nicknamed "Plantagenet".

1135 Stephen of Boulogne seizes the English throne, on the death of his uncle, Henry I.

1137-1144 St. Denis, Paris, first Gothic cathedral, is built by Abbot Suger.

Stained glass window showing Abbot Suger at St. Denis

1139 Alfonso I is first King of Portugal.

1139-1148 Civil war in England: Stephen and Mathilda struggle for the throne. Mathilda is defeated.

Mathilda, though Queen of England, was never crowned.

c.1150 Paris University is founded.

1152 Mathilda's son, Henry of Anjou, renews the struggle for the English throne.

Tomb of Eleanor of Aquitaine (1102-1169), wife of Henry of Anjou

1153 Stephen recognizes Henry of Anjou as his heir.

1154-1189 Henry of Anjou is Henry II of England and France.

1157 Malcolm IV of Scotland cedes Northumberland, Cumbria and Westmoreland to Henry II.

1159 Henry II introduces scutage, allowing knights to pay money instead of fighting in his wars.

1170 English nobleman named "Strongbow" seizes Dublin.

1170 Thomas à Becket, Archbishop of Canterbury, is killed by Henry II's knights. Becket is made a saint in **1173**.

15th century illustration of Becket's murder

1171 Henry II invades Ireland and proclaims himself Lord of Ireland.

1184 Inquisition is formed to seek out and suppress heresy (opposition to the official teaching of the Church).

1186 Constance, daughter of Roger II of Sicily, marries Emperor Henry VI.

Mosaic showing Roger II of Sicily

1189-1199 Reign of Richard I "the Lionheart" of England. He recognizes the independence of Scotland.

1199

Northern and Eastern Europe

1105 West Germans begin colonizing East Germany.

1122 Byzantines wipe out the Patzinaks in the Balkans.

1122 Concordat at Worms, Germany, ends the power struggle between the Pope and the Holy Roman Emperor.

1137-1268 Hohenstaufen dynasty rules the Holy Roman Empire.

c.1147 Moscow is founded by Kievan Prince Yuri Dolgoruky.

1147-1149 Second Crusade in complete failure, never reaching the Holy Land.

A crusader's shield had a cross on it, the sign of his promise to go to Jerusalem.

1152-1190 Reign of Frederick I Barbarossa, Holy Roman Emperor. He fights six campaigns in Italy, putting down rebellions by the Normans in southern Italy, and helping the Pope fight rebellions by the Romans in Rome.

c.1170s Serbia becomes independent from the Byzantine empire.

Map showing territory of Byzantines and Seljuk Turks in the 12th century

1171 Emperor Manuel Comnenus arrests all Venetians on Byzantine territory, but loses the resulting war with Venice.

1176 Byzantines are decisively defeated by the Seljuk Turks at Myriokephalon and lose more territory in Asia Minor.

1185-1205 Angeli dynasty rules Byzantine empire.

1186 Bulgarians rebel and establish independence from Byzantine empire.

c.1190 Teutonic Knights, a military order of monks, are founded in Germany to defend the Christian states in the Holy Land.

Map labels:
Byzantine empire in c.1180
Seljuk Turks
SERBIA
DALMATIA
THE BALKANS
BULGARIA
Black Sea
Constantinople
ASIA MINOR
Crete
Mediterranean Sea
Aleppo
Antioch
SYRIA
Damascus
Acre
HOLY LAND
Jerusalem

Africa and the Middle East

c.1100 Kingdom of Ife, West Africa, grows in importance.

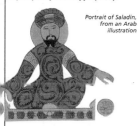

A bronze head of a ruler from Ife

1135-1269 Almohad kingdom rules much of North Africa.

1147-1149 Second Crusade fails to reach the Holy Land.

1171 Fatimids are thrown out of Egypt by Saladin, who founds the Ayyubid dynasty. He becomes ruler of Syria (**1174**) and Aleppo (**1183**).

Portrait of Saladin, from an Arab illustration

1187 Saladin, Sultan of Egypt, defeats the Christians at the Battle of Hattin and takes control of Jerusalem.

1189-1192 Third Crusade: Philippe II of France and Richard I "the Lionheart" of England fail to retake Jerusalem.

1190 A Christian named Lalibela becomes King of Ethiopia.

1191 Crusaders capture kingdom of Acre in the Holy Land.

1192 Peace of Ramlah: Saladin keeps Jerusalem, but recognizes the independence of the Christian kingdom of Acre.

The castle of Krak des Chevaliers in Syria, rebuilt by crusaders in the 12th century on the site of an earlier Islamic castle

Asia

1126-1234 Chin dynasty overruns northern China.

1127-1279 Southern Sung dynasty is established at Nanking, south China.

c.1150 Suryavarman II of Cambodia (**1112-1152**) completes the temple of Angkor Wat.

A procession at Angkor Wat

1156-1185 Civil wars in Japan between Taira, Fujiwara and Minamoto clans.

1162 Temujin, later known as Ghengis Khan, is born in Mongolia.

c.1170 Height of Srivijaya kingdom in Java under Indian Shailendra dynasty.

c.1180 Angkor empire in Cambodia is at its greatest extent.

1185 Japan: Yoshitsume Minamoto defeats the Taira clan. The Kamakura Period (**1185-1333**), named after the home district of the Minamoto.

1192 Yoritomo Minamoto is given power under the title *shogun* (hereditary military dictator). His family rules Japan until **1219**.

1193 Muhammud of Ghur conquers northern India.

The Americas

c.1100 The Toltecs arrive in the Mayan city of Chichén Itzá.

c.1100 Cahokia, at the junction of the Missouri and Mississippi rivers, is the largest town in North America.

c.1100s The Chimú peoples build large towns, including their capital Chanchan, on the north Peruvian coast. Ancestors of the Incas start to gather around Cuzco, Peru.

Map of early Central American peoples

MEXICO
Huastec
Chichén Itzá
Tula
Yucatán
Aztec
Totonac
Zapotec
Mixtec
Maya

Huari empire
San Augustín
Tiahuanaco empire
Chanchan
Moche
Chavin
Huari
Cuzco
Map of early South American settlements
Nazca
Tiahuanaco

A statue from the Temple of the Warriors, Chichén Itzá

c.1160 Chichén Itzá is invaded by tribes from the north and the Toltecs are scattered.

c.1170 Chichimec people overrun the Toltec city of Tula. The Toltec civilization is destroyed.

1179 Chichén Itzá is burned and destroyed.

c.1190 Second era of Mayan civilization begins.

Southern and Western Europe

c.1200s Rise of Gothic architecture in Europe.

Chartres Cathedral, France

Gothic window

c.1200s Flourishing of the first universities, established in Bologna (**1119**), Paris (**1150**) and Oxford (**c.1170**).

1202 Arabic numerals are introduced into Europe.

1204 Philippe II of France conquers English territory in northern France: Normandy, Maine, Anjou and Touraine.

1210-1229 Albigensian Crusade, led by Simon de Montfort the elder, against the Albigensians, a heretical sect.

1212 Battle of Las Navas de Tolosa: Christian kings of Castile, Aragon and Navarre defeat the Muslim kingdoms. Starts the break-up of the Muslim kingdoms in Spain.

1214 Battle of Bouvines: Philippe II takes all remaining English land in France, except Guyenne and Gascony.

1214-1294 Life of Roger Bacon, English monk, scholar and scientist. He carries out research into optics and is one of the first to suggest the use of lenses as spectacles.

1215 English nobles force King John to sign the *Magna Carta* ("Great Charter"), giving them the right to a Council to discuss problems. Their meetings grow to form the basis for Parliament.

An early English court meeting

1225-1274 Life of Thomas Aquinas, Italian theologian and philosopher.

c.1230 Popes begin to use inquisitors to stamp out heresy.

HERETICS

Heretics burning at the stake

The medieval Church became more and more powerful and corrupt, which led to criticism and movements for reform. Some complaints about abuses ended in attacks on the Church's authority, or official teaching. The Church condemned this as heresy. The Inquisition was set up to find and suppress heresy. People found guilty were tortured or burned. One popular heretical sect was the Cathars, known as "Albigensians" in southern France, after Albi, where they began.

1244 Albigensians are virtually wiped out after the conquest of their stronghold at Montségur, southern France.

Northern and Eastern Europe

1204 During the 4th Crusade (**1202-1204**), Crusaders sack Constantinople, depose the Byzantine emperor and set up a Latin empire, ruled by Western Roman emperors until **1258**.

1218 The ruling family in Switzerland dies out. Small independent states, called cantons, are formed.

FREDERICK II

In **1220**, Frederick II of Hohenstaufen (**1194-1250**), King of Sicily and Germany, became Holy Roman Emperor. Frederick was well-educated and lived in Sicily at the heart of a brilliant court. He reorganized the Sicilian government, making it one of the most advanced European states at the time. But his conduct and attitudes offended many. His conflict with Pope Gregory IX led to a feud between the Ghibellines (Frederick's allies) and the Guelphs (the Pope's supporters), which continued after Frederick's death, causing political chaos in Germany.

1222 Andreas II of Hungary issues the Golden Bull, giving power to the nobles and rights to the national assembly.

1224-1239 Teutonic Knights are sent by Frederick II to convert Prussians to Christianity.

1227 Denmark is defeated at Bornhöved by north German princes, who increase trade with the Baltic.

1231 German secular princes are given the same rights over territory as ecclesiastical princes.

1237-1242 Mongols invade Russia, Hungary and Poland and set up the Khanate of the Golden Horde.

1240 Battle of Neva: Russians defeat Swedes. Their general, Alexander, becomes known as "Nevsky", because of his part in the victory.

Treasure taken from Russia by the invading Mongols

1242 Alexander Nevsky defeats Teutonic Knights at Battle of Lake Peipus.

Nevsky's father's helmet

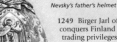

1249 Birger Jarl of Sweden conquers Finland and gives trading privileges to the Hanseatic League, an association of German and Scandinavian trading cities, led by Lübeck.

Africa and the Middle East

1200s Trans-Saharan trade continues. Ghana is in decline.

Saharan traders

1200s East Africa: trading cities, such as Kilwa, continue to flourish.

c.1200 King Lalibela of Ethiopia builds 11 churches and chapels cut into rock in the Lasta mountains, including the Church of St. George.

One of King Lalibela's churches

c.1200-1300 Mongols invade Seljuk lands.

1202-1204 Fourth Crusade.

1217-1219 Fifth Crusade.

1218 The Egyptian Ayyubid empire breaks up.

1228 Civil war in Egypt between Saladin's heirs.

1228-1229 Sixth Crusade: crusaders captured Jerusalem and Emperor Frederick II is crowned King of Jerusalem.

c.1235 Sun Diata Keita establishes kingdom of Mali, West Africa, which lasts until c.1500.

1240 Kumbi, former capital of Ghana, is destroyed.

1244 Egyptian Muslims retake Jerusalem.

1248-1254 Seventh Crusade, by Louis IX of France against Egypt.

Crusader galleon cut away to show cargo inside

Asia

c.1200-1500 First Thai kingdom, Sukhothai, is established.

1206-1526 Rule of Islamic Sultanate of Delhi, known as the Slave Dynasty: it rules most of northern India.

1211 Mongols invade China.

1218-1224 Mongols attack the empire of Khwarizm.

1221 Mongols attack Delhi.

Mongol soldiers were trained to fight on horseback

THE MONGOLS

The Mongols were warlike nomadic tribes who roamed the plains of Central Asia. In **1206**, a young Mongol warrior named Temujin was given the name Genghis Khan (meaning "supreme ruler") after uniting the tribes. Under his leadership, the Mongols began a conquest of Asia and built up a vast empire.

1227 Genghis Khan dies. His son, Ogadei is elected Great Khan (1229-1241).

1234 Mongols overthrow Chin dynasty in China.

1239 Mongols sack Ani, the capital of Armenia.

The Americas

c.1200 North America: the Mississippians dominate a wide area. They develop a remarkable culture, influenced by Mexico, building large cities on flat-topped mounds.

THE PUEBLO BUILDERS

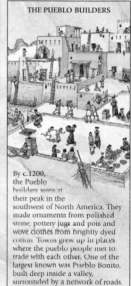

By **c.1200**, the Pueblo builders were at their peak in the southwest of North America. They made ornaments from polished stone, pottery jugs and pots and wove clothes from brightly dyed cotton. Towns grew up in places where the pueblo people met to trade with each other. One of the largest known was Pueblo Bonito, built deep inside a valley, surrounded by a network of roads. It housed around 1200 people in 800 rooms.

c.1200 The Aztecs begin to found small states in Mexico.

c.1200 The Mayan capital, Chichén Itzá, is abandoned and a new capital built at Mayapán, defended by 8 km (5 miles) of wall.

c.1200-1300 Chimú kingdom continues in Peru.

Chimú gold mummy burial mask

c.1200-1300 Beginning of the early Inca period in Peru.

Southern and Western Europe

1250

1250 The Pope gives Sicily to Charles of Anjou (in France).

1258-1282 Llewelyn of Gruffydd is Prince of Wales.

c.1258-1265 Uprising of English barons against Henry III, led by Simon de Montfort the younger. Defeated at Evesham.

Henry III of England (1207-72) being crowned at Gloucester Cathedral

1265-1321 Life of Dante Alighieri, Florentine poet and writer, famous for *La Divina Commedia* (the Divine Comedy).

1275 The English Parliament begins to meet regularly.

1282 Sicilian Vespers: Sicilians rise against their French rulers and massacre them.

1282 The death in battle of Prince Llewelyn of Wales marks the end of Welsh independence from England.

1290 Jews are expelled from England.

1290 Margaret, child Queen of Scotland, dies. Edward I of England claims the throne.

A Welsh army attacking an English castle

1295 Mateo Visconti seizes control in Milan. His dynasty rules Milan until 1447.

1295 Edward I of England calls the Model Parliament, which forms the basis for the House of Commons.

1297 French occupy Flanders (now part of Belgium).

1297 Scots, led by William Wallace, defeat the English at the Battle of Stirling Bridge.

Statue of William Wallace

1299

Northern and Eastern Europe

c.1250-1480 Mongols withdraw to southern Russia and rule the Khanate of the Golden Horde.

A Tartar soldier

1250 Collapse of imperial power in Germany and Italy, followed by the Great Interregnum (1254-1273).

1253-1278 Rule of Ottokar II of Bohemia.

1258-1282 Michael Paleologus deposes the Latin emperor in Constantinople and restores Byzantine rule.

Arabs attacking Constantinople in the 13th century, based on an early drawing

1261 Greenland is conquered by Norway.

1262-1264 Iceland comes under Norwegian rule.

1263 Norway is defeated by Scots and gives up the Hebrides islands to Scotland.

1266 Norway gives up Isle of Man to Scotland.

1273-1291 Rudolf of Habsburg is elected Holy Roman Emperor.

1278 Ottokar II of Bohemia is killed at Marchfeld. Bohemia and Moravia become estates of the Holy Roman Empire.

1280-1303 Reign of Daniel, Prince of Moscow, son of Alexander Nevsky. Under his dynasty, Moscow slowly expands in size and importance to become state of Muscovy.

1282 Rudolf of Habsburg makes his son, Albert, Duke of Austria.

1291 Three Swiss cantons (Unterwalden, Schwyz and Uri) sign the Pact of Rutli forming the Swiss Confederation.

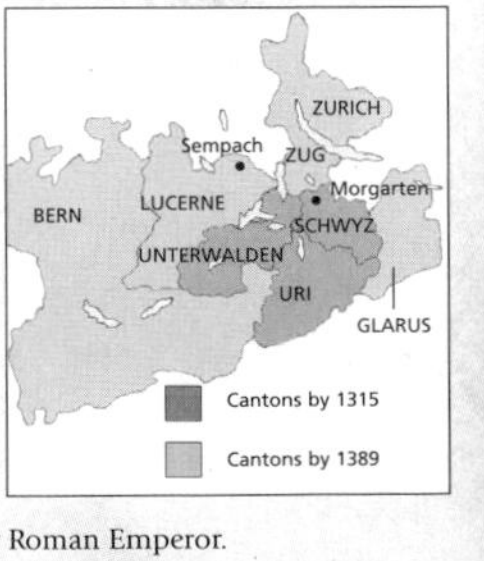
ZURICH
Sempach
ZUG
Morgarten
BERN
LUCERNE
SCHWYZ
UNTERWALDEN
URI
GLARUS
Cantons by 1315
Cantons by 1389

Map showing Swiss cantons in the 13th and 14th centuries

1293 Sweden conquers Karelia (Finland).

1298-1308 Reign of Albert I Habsburg as Holy Roman Emperor.

THE MIDDLE AGES 1250-1299

Africa and the Middle East

c.1250 Ottomans (Muslims from Turkestan) settle in northwest Turkey, working for the Seljuk Turks.

c.1250 North Africa: Berber states flourish for over 200 years. Europeans call North Africa the Barbary Coast.

1250 Mamelukes seize power and found their own military state in Egypt and remain in power until 1517.

1258 Baghdad destroyed by Mongols.

1260-1277 Reign of Mameluke Sultan Baibars of Egypt

1260 Battle of Ain Jalut, Palestine: the Mongol advance is halted by the Egyptians, led by Sultan Baibars.

13th century water clock, built for an Arab sultan. Every hour the bird whistled.

1262-1263 Baibars conquers the Ayyubid lands in Syria.

1265-1271 Baibars takes most of the Christian kingdom of Outremer in the Holy Land.

1268 Baibars captures Antioch, Anatolia.

1270-1291 Eighth and last Crusade, led by Louis IX of France, who dies in Tunis, North Africa.

1281-1326 Reign of Osman I, *emir* (chief) of a small Turkish princedom. In 1301, he declares himself Sultan of the Turks and becomes the founder of the Ottoman empire.

Osman I

1291 Egyptian Mamelukes take Acre, the last stronghold of Outremer. The end of the Crusades.

Asia

1251-1265 Hulagu, grandson of Genghis Khan, conquers Persia and sets up the Il-Khan empire, which survives until 1336.

1259-1294 Kublai Khan takes over as Great Khan, ruling the Eastern Khanate

1271-1295 Marco Polo of Venice travels overland to China. From 1275-1292, he works for Mongol ruler Kublai Khan.

1274-1281 Unsuccessful Mongol invasion of Japan.

1279 Kublai Khan founds the Yuan dynasty in China. Mongol empire is now at its largest.

Kublai Khan

1280 Kublai Khan overthrows the Sung dynasty. Yuan dynasty rules all China until 1368.

1281 Second attempted invasion of Japan by Mongols. The Japanese attack the Mongol fleet and capture several ships, the rest of the fleet is scattered by *kamikaze* ("divine winds").

Japanese woodcut showing a Mongol ship under attack

1290-1325 Firuz, a Turkish Muslim, founds the Khalji dynasty in Delhi, India. Islam starts to spread south to the Deccan.

1293 The first Christian missionaries reach China.

The Americas

1250

INUIT

ATHABASCANS

MISSISSIPPI MOUND BUILDERS

PUEBLO BUILDERS

American peoples 1200 - 1500

Chichén Itzá

Tenochtitlán

Yucatán peninsula

AZTECS

MAYA

• Quito

CHIMÚ

INCA

• Cuzco

1299

Southern and Western Europe

1301 Wales becomes the principality of the heir to the English throne.

1302 Flemish craftsmen seize power from wealthy pro-French merchant guilds. They fight and defeat the French army at the Battle of Courtrai, but are beaten at Cassel.

1306 Jews are expelled from France.

1307-1314 Knights Templars, a military religious order, are investigated for heresy.

1309-1378 Pope's court moves to Avignon, France.

1314 Robert Bruce, King of Scotland (**1306-1329**) defeats the English at the Battle of Bannockburn.

1317 Salic Law in France bans women from inheriting the throne.

1323 The Declaration of Arbroath sets the wishes of Scotland's people above those of the Scottish kings.

1328 Valois dynasty begins in France.

1328 Edward II accepts Scotland's independence.

THE HUNDRED YEARS' WAR

The Hundred Years' War is the name given to the struggle between England and France, which lasted from **1337-1453**. Ever since **1066**, there had been wars between them over land held in France by the English kings. This time, war broke out when the English king, Edward III, claimed the French throne itself. The English made early gains, winning battles at Sluys (**1340**), Crécy (**1346**), Calais (**1347**) and Poitiers (**1356**), when they took the French king captive. By the Treaty of Brétigny (**1360**), they won large areas of France, but hostilities soon broke out again. By the end of the war in **1453**, the English kept only Calais and the Channel islands.

Edward III of England and his coat of arms, which included the fleur-de-lis, symbol of the French kings

THE BLACK DEATH

1347-1353 The Black Death, a bubonic plague carried by fleas on black rats, reaches Genoa, Italy from the East via the Crimea. It sweeps through Europe, killing as many as 20 million people - one person in three.

Trying to stop the spread of infection by burning the clothes of plague victims

Northern and Eastern Europe

1301 The Arpad dynasty comes to an end in Hungary.

1306 King Wenceslas III of Hungary and Bohemia is murdered. The Premsyl dynasty dies out.

Hungarian coat-of-arms

1308 Henry VII of Luxembourg becomes Holy Roman Emperor until **1313**.

1310 John of Luxembourg inherits Bohemia.

1315 Battle of Morgarten: Swiss peasants repulse an attack by the army of Leopold I of Austria.

1320 Vladislav Lokiekek becomes King of Poland and restores Polish unity.

1328-1340 Moscow grows under Duke Ivan I. It becomes the residence of the Metropolitan, the head of the Orthodox Church in Russia.

Muscovite artists painted religious pictures, called icons, usually on wooden panels. This one is of St. Michael.

1333-1370 Casimir III "the Great" strengthens Poland.

1342-1382 Reign of Louis the Great of Hungary. He conquers Croatia, Serbia, Bosnia, Wallachia, Bulgaria, Transylvania and Moldavia.

1343 Teutonic Knights acquire Estonia from Denmark.

A Teutonic knight

Territory held by the Teutonic Knights

1346 Golden age of Bohemia and city of Prague begins with the reign of Charles IV of the Luxembourg dynasty.

Africa and the Middle East

c.1300 The empire of Benin emerges in Nigeria.

c.1312-1337 Mansa Musa rules Mali.

Mansa Musa, from a 14th century map

1324 Mansa Musa, King of Mali, goes on pilgrimage to Mecca. He visits Cairo and impresses everyone with his wealth.

Cairo city gates, built during the Fatimid rule

1325 Ibn Batuta, a Moroccan Muslim, travels to Mecca, Arabia, via Egypt, Jerusalem and Damascus.

Ibn Battuta used Arabic script and probably had writing materials like these.

Asia

c.1300 Ghazan, Mongol ruler of Persia, declares Islam the state religion.

1307 The first Catholic archbishop is established in Beijing, China.

c.1325 No plays develop in Japan: classic Japanese drama, using music and dancing.

No masks of a young girl and the devil

1325-1351 Reign of Mohammed Ibn Tughluk, Sultan of Delhi. He expands his territories and briefly conquers the Deccan (South India).

Tower built by the first Sultan of Delhi, to celebrate his victories

1333 China suffers drought, famine, floods, and plague. Five million die.

1333 Kamakura shogunate ends in Japan. Emperor Go-daigo rules without a shogun (1333-1336).

1336 The Il-Khan empire is replaced by a Turcoman dynasty.

1336-1565 India: the Hindu empire of Vijayanagar becomes a base for resistance to Islam. It is dominant in southern India by **c.1370**.

1349 Earliest Chinese settlement in Singapore.

The Americas

c.1300 Constant warfare among the Maya people in Yucatán contributes to the decline of their civilization.

The quetzal bird, sacred to the Aztecs

c.1300 North America: Pueblo building ends abruptly, possibly as a result of drought and the arrival of Athabascan Indians migrating from the northwest. By **c.1500**, they have completely taken over the southwest.

c.1300 The Inca people settle around Cuzco in Peru.

c.1300 The Aztec people arrive in the Valley of Mexico.

THE RISE OF THE AZTECS

From **c.1325**, the Aztecs built up a large, well-organized empire in Mexico. They were a great warrior people, but their culture was also highly sophisticated in many areas, especially science, art, architecture and agriculture. The Aztecs had strict laws and complex religious beliefs and ceremonies. The city of Tenochtitlán, built by a group led by Chief Tenoch, on islands in Lake Texcoco, became the residence of the major tribe.

Aztec warrior

Map of Aztec territory at its peak c.1519

CENTRAL AMERICA · Texcoco · Tenochtitlán · Aztec · Gulf of Mexico · PACIFIC OCEAN

c.1335 Tenochtitlán is increased in size by the building of floating gardens in the lake.

This is what an Aztec temple might have looked like.

Southern and Western Europe

c.1350 The Renaissance begins in Italy.

c.1350 The first firearms, muzzle-loading cannon, are used in Europe.

1355 Revolt against taxes in Paris, led by cloth merchant Etienne Marcel.

1358 The Jacquerie: French peasants rebel against harsh conditions, but are defeated by nobles and merchants.

1363-1404 Philippe the Good, son of King Jean II of France, is made Duke of Burgundy.

1367 Civil war in Castile, Spain. France and England back opposite sides.

1371 House of Stewart rules in Scotland.

1373 Treaty of Anglo-Portuguese friendship.

THE GREAT SCHISM

In **1296** and **1302**, Pope Boniface VIII issued two documents, called bulls, banning churchmen from paying taxes to kings and declaring the authority of the Catholic Church. This led to conflict. Philippe IV of France imprisoned Boniface and set up a papal court in Avignon, France, electing a French pope. In **1378**, Urban VI was also elected pope and established a rival court in Rome. This period, known as the Great Schism, lasted until **1417**.

Bishop's staff

1378 Unsuccessful uprising of *ciompi* (clothworkers) in Florence, Italy.

c.1380 John Wycliffe preaches that the Bible alone is the authority for Christian belief. The Church condemns his teachings and his followers, the Lollards, are persecuted.

1381 Jack Straw and Wat Tyler lead English peasants in a march to London to protest against living and working conditions. They disperse after the King agrees to some of their demands.

1381 Venice defeats Genoa after a hundred years of war.

1382 Uprising in Paris, France, against taxes.

1387 Geoffrey Chaucer (**c.1345-1400**), the first great poet to write in English, writes *The Canterbury Tales*.

Revolting peasants

Northern and Eastern Europe

1354 Turks acquire Gallipoli, their first European possession.

1355 Charles IV of Bohemia becomes Holy Roman Emperor and reigns until **1378**.

Charles IV's crown

15th century Prague

1361 Denmark is defeated by the Hanseatic League.

1370 Lithuanians are defeated at the Battle of Rudan by the Teutonic Knights.

1370 Hungary and Poland are unified under the Hungarian king, Louis of Anjou.

1370 Peace of Stralsund between Denmark and the Hanseatic League. The League's power is at its height.

1373 The Byzantine emperor becomes an Ottoman vassal (subordinate to the Ottoman empire).

1380 Muscovites defeat Mongols at the Battle of Kulikova.

Prince Dimitri of Moscow and his army at the Battle of Kulikova

1386 Union of Poland and Lithuania.

1389 Battle of Kosovo: Turks gain control of the Balkans.

1397 The Union of Kalmar unites Scandinavia under Margaret, Queen of Denmark and Norway (**1387-1412**).

Africa and the Middle East

c.1350 Fortress at Great Zimbabwe, southern Africa, is at its largest.

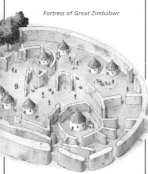

Fortress of Great Zimbabwe

c.1350-1600 Kingdom of Songhai in West Africa.

1352-1355 Ibn Batuta travels in West Africa and visits Mali and writes an account of all he sees. He reaches Timbuktu in 1353. From the writings of other Arab scholars, and archaeology, other African states from this period are known: Kanem-Bornu, Kongo and Benin.

Ibn Batuta welcomed by Indian prince

1375 Mamelukes conquer Sis, Armenia: the end of Armenian independence.

c.1380-1662 Kongo kingdom in Central Africa.

1397 Portuguese explorers reach the Canary Islands.

Asia

c.1350 Cultural peak of the Majapahit empire in Java.

TAMERLANE

From 1369-1405, a Mongol chief named Tamerlane began to build a new empire, from his base at Samarkand. He seized land in Persia, Russia and India, conquering Herat in 1381, destroying Delhi in 1398-1399 and annexing the Punjab. But the empire did not last long after his death.

Tamerlane

1368 The Yuan dynasty in China is overthrown and replaced by the native Chinese Ming dynasty, founded by a Buddhist monk named Chu Yuan-chang, also known as Hung Wu.

Ming porcelain

1369 Thais invade Cambodia.

1392-1636 Great age of the Choson dynasty in Korea.

1394 Temple of the Golden Pavilion is built, near Kyoto, Japan.

Chinese junk

The Americas

c.1352 Acamapitzin is elected first King of the Aztecs in Mexico.

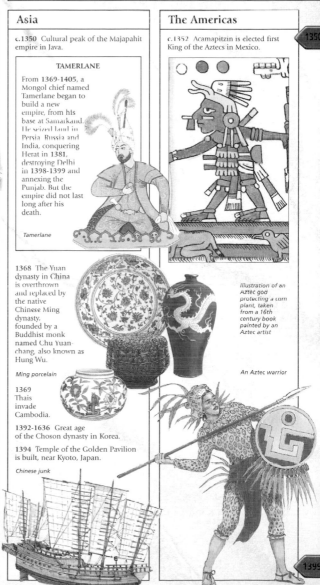

Illustration of an Aztec god protecting a corn plant, taken from a 16th century book painted by an Aztec artist

An Aztec warrior

1350

1399

Southern and Western Europe

1400

1400-1415 Rebellion of Owen Glendower in Wales.

1407 Casi di San Georgio, the first European public bank, is established in Genoa, Italy.

1410-1411 Civil war in France.

1415 Henry V of England defeats French at Agincourt.

1416 Henry the Navigator, Prince of Portugal founds a school of navigation. He encourages expeditions **c.1420-1460**.

1422-1461 Henry VI is King of England.

1429 Jeanne d'Arc, a French peasant girl, drives the English out of Orléans, France. Burned as a witch in **1431**.

1434 Cosimo de' Medici takes control of Florence, Italy. The Medici dynasty rules Florence until **1737**.

Henry the Navigator

1442 Alfonso of Aragon conquers Naples.

1447 French Orléans family claims Milan by inheritance.

THE RENAISSANCE

The Renaissance means "rebirth". It is the name given to the renewed interest in the art, architecture and learning of Classical Greece and Rome, which inspired people to try out new ideas, and marked the end of the Middle Ages and the beginning of modern times. The movement began in Italy in the 14th century, and eventually influenced all of Europe, reaching its height in the 15th and 16th centuries. The most powerful patrons of the Renaissance were the Medici, a family of Florentine bankers, who encouraged artists and scholars to work in their city. Florence was the home of great artists such as Leonardo da Vinci (**1452-1519**) and Michelangelo Buonarroti (**1475-1564**), architects such as Filippo Brunelleschi (**1377-1446**) and writers such as Dante Alighieri (**1265-1321**).

Lorenzo de' Medici leading a procession through the city of Florence

Northern and Eastern Europe

1410 Poles defeat the Teutonic Knights at Tannenberg.

1415 John Hus (**1372-1415**), a Bohemian religious reformer, is condemned by the Church Council of Constance and burned as a heretic.

1415 Frederick VI of Hohenzollern becomes Frederick I, Elector of Brandenburg.

1416 Venetians defeat the Turks off Gallipoli, Turkey.

1419-1436 Hussite wars between Bohemia and Moravia and the Holy Roman Empire triggered by the death of John Hus.

Mount Tabor castle, a Hussite stronghold

1422 First siege of Constantinople by the Ottoman Turks. Sultan Murat I invades Greece.

1430 Murat I of Turkey conquers Thessalonika, Greece.

1437 Albert II Habsburg of Austria becomes King of Hungary and Bohemia, and is elected King of Germany in **1438-1439**. The Habsburgs are king-emperors until **1918**.

1439 Russian and Greek Orthodox Churches are formally separated.

1449

1400

Africa and the Middle East

c.1400s Chinese traders join Arab and Indian merchants trading in East Africa.

East African traders

1401 Tamerlane conquers Damascus (in Syria) and Baghdad (in Iraq).

1415 Portuguese conquer Ceuta, North Africa.

1419 Portuguese reach Madeira.

c.1420 Chinese are believed to have rounded Cape of Good Hope (South Africa).

15th century Chinese map showing Cape of Good Hope

c.1430 Massive stone buildings are erected at Great Zimbabwe.

1431 Portuguese reach the Azores.

1434 Portuguese courtier Gil Eannes sails around Cape of Bojador, near Canary Islands, after several failed Portuguese attempts.

Portugese ship

Asia

1403-1424 Reign of Yung-Lo, one of the greatest Ming emperors of China.

Emperor Yung Lo

1405-1433 Chinese courtier, Cheng Ho, with a fleet of 317 ships and 27,000 men, makes seven great voyages. He visits Indochina, Indonesia, Siam (Thailand), the Maldives, Borneo, the Persian Gulf, Arabia and East Africa.

1421 Beijing becomes the capital of China.

```
CHINA
                    Beijing
        Ch'ang-an

    ☐ Tang empire
    — Border of Sung empire
    — Border of Ming empire
    — Silk Road (trade route
       to the West)
```

Map of China in the Middle Ages

1424 King of Siam dies. His two eldest sons fight each other for the throne on elephants and both die.

Battling on elephants

1428 Chinese are expelled from Vietnam.

The Americas

c.1400s Peru: Viracocha Inca (8th emperor) takes the title Sapa Inca, meaning "Supreme Inca".

c.1420s Mexico: a causeway is built from the Aztec island city of Tenochtitlán to the mainland. Emperor Itzcoatl adopts an aggressive policy toward local tribes. He forces them to pay tribute and establishes a three-city league with Texcoco and Tlacopán, to gain political control of the region.

c.1436-1464 Rule of Emperor Montezuma I of the Aztecs.

THE INCA EMPIRE

The Late Inca (or Empire) Period in Peru began with the reign of Pachacuti Inca (1438-1471), who started conquering an empire from his capital Cuzco. He was regarded as half-god, half-human. The Incas had a well-developed social system. Everyone had to work in accordance with their rank and ability. In return, orphans, the sick and elderly were looked after. The Incas were also expert stonemasons and farmers, and built good roads across very difficult, rough land.

An Inca knife

Inca warriors

1449

39

Southern and Western Europe

1450 Francesco Sforza becomes Duke of Milan.

1452-1519 Life of Leonardo da Vinci, Florentine artist.

THE WAR OF THE ROSES

The Wars of the Roses (1455-1485) is the name given to the struggle between two rival families for the English crown: York, whose emblem was a white rose, and Lancaster, whose emblem was a red rose. Henry VI of Lancaster (**1422-1461**), was only a child when he became king and proved incompetent when he came of age. Richard, Duke of York, was made Protector in **1454**, but in **1455** he was excluded from the Royal Council and fighting broke out. The wars ended in **1485**, with the victory of Henry Tudor, who became Henry VII (**1485-1603**) first king of the Tudor dynasty.

Henry Tudor's army

1461-1483 Edward IV is King of England.

1462-1492 Lorenzo de' Medici ("the Magnificent") rules Florence.

1469 Ferdinand of Aragon marries Isabella of Castile.

1477 Charles the Bold, Duke of Burgundy, is killed. His daughter Marie marries Maximilian Habsburg of Austria.

1477-1493 France and Austria fight over Burgundian lands.

1479 Ferdinand of Aragon succeeds his father as King of Aragon and unites the kingdom with Castile.

1483 Charles VIII of France claims Naples.

1483 Edward V is King of England, but not crowned.

1483-1485 Richard III is King of England.

1485 The Battle of Bosworth ends the War of the Roses in England. Henry Tudor becomes Henry VII, first king of the Tudor dynasty.

1487 Rebellion in England by Lambert Simnel, who claims to be the nephew of Edward IV.

1492 Ferdinand and Isabella conquer Granada, the last Muslim kingdom in Spain.

1493 Maximilian Habsburg becomes Holy Roman Emperor. Peace of Senlis: Burgundy is divided between France and the Empire.

1494-1495 France invades Italy and is driven back. Start of a struggle for power between France and the Habsburgs.

1497 Rebellion in England by Perkin Warbeck who claims to be the son of Edward IV.

1498 Louis XII of France invades Italy and takes Milan.

Northern and Eastern Europe

1453 Ottoman Turks capture Constantinople: the Byzantine empire finally comes to an end.

Mehmet II, the Ottoman sultan, marching his troops through the city of Constantinople after their victory

1455 Johann Gutenberg develops printing presses and publishes the Gutenberg Bible, the first printed book in Europe.

Gutenberg and a page from his Bible

THE FIRST TSARS

Ivan III ("the Great") of Moscow (**1462-1505**) extended his territory and in **1478** conquered Novgorod, the old Russian capital. In **1480**, he liberated Moscow from Mongol rule and declared himself first Tsar (sole ruler) of Russia. Ivan married a Byzantine princess and adopted many Byzantine customs. Russia continued to grow under his son, Vassily, and grandson, Ivan IV "the Terrible".

St. Basil's Cathedral, Moscow, built by Ivan IV

1456-1467 Ottoman Turks take over Balkan states.

1468-1469 Denmark pawns Orkney and Shetland to Scotland.

1471-1480 Ottoman Turks raid Styria (in Austria).

1488 South German cities, knights and princes establish the Swabian League, to preserve peace within the Empire.

1499 Swiss independence is recognized at the Peace of Basle.

Africa and the Middle East

c.1450 Portuguese start trading in West Africa.

1451-1481 Reign of Ottoman Turkish Sultan Mehmet II, known as "the Conqueror", after his conquest of Constantinople in 1453.

Mehmet II

1461 Portuguese reach Sierra Leone, West Africa.

1463-1479 Ottoman Turks are at war with Venice.

1464-1492 Reign of Sunni Ali, ruler of Songhai in West Africa, who conquers Timbuktu and expands his empire at the expense of Mali.

1471 Portuguese conquer Tangier, Morocco.

1482 Portuguese establish a fort at El Mina on the Gold Coast (Ghana).

1487-1488 Portuguese navigator, Bartholomeu Dias, rounds the Cape of Good Hope, South Africa.

This European map of 1489 shows a little knowledge of the West African coast

1490 King Nzinga Nkuwu of the Kongo becomes a Christian.

1493 Songhai empire in West Africa reaches its peak.

The city of Timbuktu

Asia

1451-1489 Rule of Bahlol Lodi, the first Pathan king of Delhi.

1467-1477 Onin War in Japan between rival clans.

1469-1539 Life of Guru Nanak, who founds the Sikh religion in c.1500.

The Sikh flag   *Guru Nanak*

1471 Vietnamese expand south.

1477-1568 Provincial wars in Japan, ending with the victory of Oda Nobunaga.

1494 Babar, a descendent of Genghis Khan and Tamerlane, becomes Prince of Ferghana, Central Asia.

Babar

1497-1499 Vasco da Gama, a Portuguese navigator in search of trade, makes the first sea voyage by a European to India and back. Da Gama met hostility on the East African coast, where trade was controlled by Arabs.

Da Gama's ship being attacked

The Americas

1460 Mayapan is destroyed: the Mayan civilization comes to an end.

1471-1493 Reign of Emperor Topa Inca, who extends the empire south.

c.1476 Incas conquer the Chimú kingdom in Peru.

1492-1493 Christopher Columbus reaches Bahamas and West Indies, while sailing west in search of a route to the East Indies.

Columbus setting off for the West Indies

1493-1525 Reign of Huayna Capac, the greatest Inca conqueror. He founds a second capital at Quito.

1494 Treaty of Tordesillas: Pope Alexander VI fixes a line to divide spheres of influence in America between Spain and Portugal.

SOUTH AMERICA

Quito

Cuzco

Portuguese influence

Expansion of the Inca empire in Peru

- Under Pachacuti to 1463
- Pachacuti and Topa Inca, to 1471
- Topa Inca, to 1493

Spanish influence

1497 John Cabot, an Italian explorer employed by Henry VII of England, reaches Newfoundland, Canada.

1498 Christopher Columbus reaches Trinidad and the coast of Venezuela.

1499-1502 Amerigo Vespucci, a Florentine navigator, explores the South American coast.

Amerigo Vespucci

1450

1499

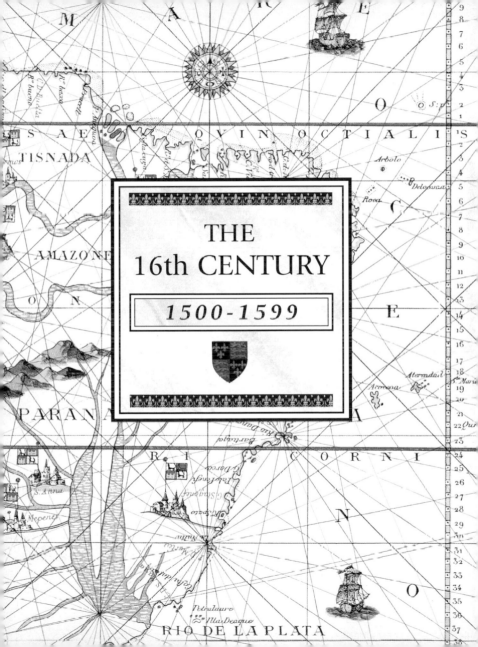

THE
16th CENTURY

1500-1599

Southern and Western Europe

1501 Louis XII of France conquers Naples, Italy.

1509-1547 Reign of King Henry VIII of England.

1510 Holy League formed to drive France from Italy.

1512 French invade Milan, but are defeated and expelled from Italy.

1512 Ferdinand II of Castile annexes Navarre.

Henry VIII's coat-of-arms

1513 Battle of Flodden between England and Scotland. James IV of Scotland is killed.

1513 Niccolò Machiavelli (**1469-1527**), a Florentine statesman, writes *The Prince*, advocating ruthlessness and cunning in order to achieve political success.

THE EMPIRE OF CHARLES V

In the early 16th century, Europe was dominated by the vast empire of Charles V (**1500-1558**), of the Austrian Habsburg family. He became King of Spain in **1516** and was elected Holy Roman Emperor in **1519**, making him the most powerful monarch in Europe. He defeated his great rival, François I of France, after five wars in Italy, and stopped the advance of the Ottoman Turks. Spain prospered, because of the riches discovered in the New World (America). But there were social and economic difficulties in Germany, as well as religious turmoil caused by the Reformation (see opposite). In **1521**, Charles divided his empire, giving Austria to his brother Ferdinand. In **1556**, Charles abdicated, splitting the empire between his brother Ferdinand and his son, Philip II.

Charles V

1515-1547 Reign of François I of France. He defeats the Swiss at the Battle of Marignano (**1515**) and conquers Milan, Italy.

Coffee beans

1516 Coffee is first imported from America.

1520 Field of the Cloth of Gold: peace talks between Henry VIII and François I.

1520 Chocolate is imported from America.

1521 Silk-making begins in France.

1521-1544 Four wars between Charles V and the French in Italy.

Northern and Eastern Europe

1513 Scandinavia: the Union of Kalmar ends.

1516 The Netherlands comes under Spanish control, with the accession of Charles I of Spain.

THE REFORMATION

The Reformation began as an attempt to reform the Catholic Church, but it provoked a religious upheaval that led to the creation of Protestant churches and a split in Christian Europe. It was triggered by Martin Luther (**1483-1546**), a monk and professor of theology at Wittenburg in Germany, who believed that religious beliefs should be based on the Bible, rather than the teachings of the Church. In **1517**, he nailed his 95 theses (proposals for change) to a church door. As a result, he was declared a heretic at the Diet of Worms (a council held by the Emperor), in **1521**. Luther went into hiding, and developed his ideas for a Lutheran Church. Lutheranism won followers in several German states, provoking quarrels and wars between them and German Catholic states.

The Cathedral at Worms

1519 Inspired by Luther, Ulrich Zwingli (**1484-1531**) begins preaching church reform in Zurich. In **1523** he writes 67 theses, suggesting changes in religious belief, and church organization. These are accepted by the city council. His ideas spread through South Germany and Switzerland.

Mercenary soldier, or landsknecht, employed by the Emperor

1519 Charles I, King of Spain, is elected Holy Roman Emperor, Charles V.

1521 Belgrade, Serbia, falls to the Ottoman Turks.

1522-1523 The imperial knights rebel against their overlord, the Archbishop of Trier, in protest against their declining economic and social position.

1523 Sweden gains independence from Denmark. Vasa dynasty begins with the reign of Gustav I (**1523-1560**).

1523 German Imperial knights are defeated by an alliance of princes at the Battle of Landstuhl.

1524-1525 Peasants rise up against their landlords in South and Central Germany.

Africa and the Middle East

1500 Mohammed Turre (1494-1528) of Songhai expands his territory in West Africa.

1502 Safavid dynasty is established in Persia (now Iran) by Ismail I.

1504 Nubians destroy the Christian kingdom of Meroë (now Sudan).

1504-1546 Reign of the Christian King Afonso of the Kongo.

1505 Songhai people invade Mali.

1505-1507 Portuguese establish forts on the East African coast.

1508 Portuguese set up a factory in Mozambique.

1509 Spain takes Oran, North Africa.

1513 Portuguese establish posts at Sena and Tete on the Zambezi river.

1514 Turks fight the Persians.

1516-1518 Selim conquers North Iraq, Syria and Palestine.

1517 Turks conquer Egypt.

1518 First full cargo of slaves sails from Guinea to the New World.

THE OTTOMAN TURKS

The great age of the Ottoman Turks was in the 16th century, especially during the reign of Suleiman "the Magnificent" **(1520-1566)**. Under him the Turkish empire took control of Egypt, parts of North Africa, and most of the Middle East. They also held land in the Balkans, in Eastern Europe.

When they captured Constantinople, the Ottomans added minarets (towers) to the Church of St Sophia, converting it into a mosque.

Asia

1504 Babar becomes Master of Kabul, Afghanistan.

Babar, the first Mogul

1510 Portuguese annex Goa, on the west coast of India.

1511 Portuguese take control in Malacca, Malaya.

1514 Portuguese reach China. By 1516, they are trading from Canton.

1519-1522 The first circumnavigation of the World is led by Ferdinand Magellan, a Portuguese navigator, sponsored by Emperor Charles V. Magellan was heading for the Molucca islands in the East Indies, which were rich in spices, by sailing west around the tip of South America.

1521 Magellan reaches the Molucca islands, but is killed in the Philippines; one of his captains continues to sail west back to Europe.

1523 European traders are expelled from Chinese ports.

Chinese boat called a junk

The Americas

1500 Aztec empire reaches its greatest extent under Ahuizotl.

1501 Anglo-Portuguese expedition to Newfoundland.

1504 Amerigo Vespucci, a Florentine navigator, describes his voyages to South America. His discoveries are known as the New World.

c.1507 The New World becomes known as America.

1510 The first African slaves are brought to America.

1513 Ponce de León, a Spanish explorer, discovers Florida.

1513 Nuñez de Balboa, a Spanish explorer, crosses the Isthmus of Panama and finds the Pacific Ocean.

THE CONQUEST OF MEXICO AND PERU

The early explorers of the New World returned with stories of the great wealth to be found. Spanish fortune-hunters, known as conquistadors, followed in search of gold and land. The most famous were Hernando Cortés, who conquered Mexico between **1519-1521**, and Francisco Pizarro, who conquered Peru between **1532-1534**. The Spanish conquerors came into conflict with two great native warrior civilizations - the Aztecs of Mexico and the Incas of Peru. But the Spaniards had the advantage of horses and cannons and these civilizations were soon destroyed

Aztec carving showing stars and planets

1520 Ferdinand Magellan, Portuguese navigator, finds the Magellan Straits.

1521-1549 Spaniards colonize Venezuela

1500

1524

Southern and Western Europe

1525 Battle of Pavia: Spain defeats France and François I is taken prisoner. England and France make peace with Spain.

1527 Charles V's troops sack Rome and capture Pope Clement VII.

1527-1530 The Medici family is expelled from Florence.

1529 Peace of Cambrai: France renounces claim to Italy and Charles V renounces his claim to the lost Burgundian lands.

1530 The Knights Hospitallers, a military religious order founded during the Crusades, establish a base in Malta.

1531 The Inquisition is established in Portugal.

1534 Henry VIII of England declares himself supreme head of the English Church.

1536 The English and Welsh governments are unified.

1541 John Knox starts the Reformation in Scotland.

1542 Mary Stuart (1542-1587) becomes Queen of Scotland, at the age of one week.

1543 Andreas Vesalius, a pharmacist from Brussels, is the first scholar to make a detailed study of the human body.

1543 Alliance of Henry VIII of England and Charles V of Spain against France and Scotland.

King Henry VIII

1544 Peace of Crespi ends wars between France and Spain in Italy.

1547 English invade Scotland and defeat Scots at the Battle of Pinkie. Mary, Queen of Scots, is sent to France to marry the Dauphin (the heir to the throne).

1547-1559 Reign of Henri II of France.

THE COUNTER REFORMATION

To fight the Reformation, the Catholic Church set up colleges to train priests to win back Protestants and make new converts. The Jesuits, founded by Ignatius Loyola in 1534, acted as teachers and missionaries, as far away as India and Japan. In 1545, the Council of the Catholic Church met at Trent, North Italy, launching an energetic campaign. They reinstated the Inquisition, and Protestants were condemned and burned as heretics. The Baroque movement in the arts also helped to attract converts, with its flamboyant style of painting, music and architecture.

The piazza of St. Peter's, Rome, built in the Baroque style in 1656-1667 by Bernini

1547-1553 Reign of Edward VI of England.

Northern and Eastern Europe

1525 Albert of Hohenzollern, ruler of Prussia, becomes a Lutheran and secularizes the state.

1526 Battle of Mohacs: Louis II of Hungary is defeated and killed by the Ottoman Turks. Charles V's brother, Ferdinand, and John Zapolya are both elected kings of Hungary.

1529 Ottoman Turks besiege Vienna, Austria.

1529 Second Diet of Speyer, Germany.

1529 War between Swiss Catholics and Protestants.

1530 Charles V is crowned Holy Roman Emperor by the Pope: the last imperial coronation by a pope.

1531 The Protestant League of Schmalkalden is formed.

1531 Copernicus (1473-1543), a Polish astronomer, circulates his revolutionary theory, demonstrating that the planets move around the Sun, not around the Earth as the Church had taught.

1532 Peace of Nuremburg: Protestants in the Holy Roman Empire are allowed to follow their religion.

1532-1533 War between Turkey and Austria over Hungary.

1533-1584 Reign of Ivan IV ("the Terrible") in Russia.

1534-1535 Münster in northern Germany is taken over by Anabaptists, religious sects who deny the need for government.

Diagram showing Copernicus's idea of the universe

JOHN CALVIN

Jean Cauvin (1509-1564), usually known as John Calvin, was another leading figure of the Reformation. Based in Geneva, Switzerland, he published *Institutes* in 1536, containing his ideas for reform, which became the basis for a new religion: Calvinism. In 1541, Calvin began organizing the Church in Geneva. It was to be self-governing, electing pastors (to preach), doctors (to decide on matters of faith), elders (to enforce discipline) and deacons (to care for the poor). A committee, called a synod, arranged elections. Although Calvinism was stricter than Lutheranism, it was better organized and won many converts.

1541-1688 Hungary becomes a province of the Ottomans.

1547 Charles V defeats League of Schmalkalden at Battle of Muhlberg.

1547 Ivan IV (right) takes the title "Tsar of all the Russias".

Africa and the Middle East

1535 Charles V of Spain conquers Tunis, North Africa.

1538 Ottoman Turks capture Aden.

1543 Ethiopian Christians, helped by Portugal, repel the Muslim advance into Ethiopia.

Ethiopian Christian crosses

1545 Ottoman Turks occupy Ethiopian city of Massawa and complete their occupation of the rest of Ethiopia.

Bronze figures from Mali

1546 The Songhai people destroy the Mali empire in West Africa.

1549-1582 Reign of Askia David, King of Songhai.

Asia

THE MOGUL EMPIRE

The Muslim Mogul empire was founded by Babar, Prince of Ferghana in Afghanistan, a descendent of the Mongol Tamerlane. He invaded the Punjab in 1526 and defeated the Sultan of Delhi at the Battle of Panipat, and gradually established control, winning battles at Kanwaha in 1527 and Gogra in 1529. Babar's grandson, Akbar (1556-1605) extended Mogul control over most of central and northern India. Akbar was a wise ruler, who attempted to unite his subjects culturally, as well as by conquest, by allowing religious toleration. Indian culture flourished during his reign, producing great works of art, architecture and poetry.

The Koran

1533 North Vietnam splits into Tongking and Annam.

1539 Burmese kingdom of Toungoo conquers Mons kingdom of Pegu.

1540 Babar's son, Humayun, is driven out of India by the Afghan Sher Shah.

1542 Francis Xavier, a Portuguese Jesuit missionary, arrives in Goa, on the west coast of India.

1545 Humayun captures Kabul, Afghanistan.

1549-1551 Francis Xavier and his missionaries spread Christianity in Japan and participate in trade.

The Americas

1526 John Cabot, Italian explorer, sails to the River Plate, Argentina.

1528 Germans attempt to colonize Venezuela.

1530 Portuguese begin to colonize Brazil.

1531 Rio de Janeiro, Brazil, is founded.

1534 French expedition, led by Jacques Cartier, reaches Labrador, Canada.

1535 Buenos Aires, Argentina, and Lima, Peru, are founded.

1535 Jacques Cartier discovers the St. Lawrence River, and sails to the site of Montreal, Canada.

Jacques Cartier

1535-1538 Gonzalo Jimenez de Quesada, a Spanish conquistador, conquers Colombia.

1536 Jesuits found Asunción, Paraguay.

1536 Inca rebellion in Peru, led by Manco Inca. He rules from Villcabamba until 1545, when the Inca Empire comes to an end.

1540-1544 Pedro de Valdivia, a Spanish conquistador, explores Chile.

1541 American Indian revolt in Mexico.

North American moose

1542 Spanish explorer Francisco de Orellana sails along the Amazon river.

1542 Charles V's New Laws abolish native slavery in Spanish colonies and limit the colonists' control.

1545 Silver discovered in Peru.

1548 Silver discovered in Mexico.

Silver llamas made of Peruvian silver

Southern and Western Europe

1550

1552-1556 War between Henri II of France and Charles V of Spain.

1553 Tobacco first introduced into Europe, from America via Spain.

1553-1558 Reign of Mary I of England. She marries Philip II of Spain and England returns to Catholicism. 300 Protestants are burned.

Mary I

1555 Charles V abdicates. His son becomes Philip II of Spain, and inherits Habsburg land in Italy, Netherlands and America.

1558 England loses Calais to France.

1558-1603 Reign of Elizabeth I of England. She reinstates the Anglican Church.

1559 Henri II of France dies. His widow, Mary, Queen of Scots, returns to Scotland from France.

1559 Jean Nicot first imports tobacco into France from America. The word nicotine is named after him.

1559 Treaty of Cateau-Cambrésis: peace between France and Spain.

THE FRENCH WARS OF RELIGION

By the mid-16th century, rival factions of French Protestants (called Huguenots) and Catholics had emerged at the French Court. A succession of weak kings failed to keep their rivalry in check and the result was a series of bloody civil wars, which lasted from **1562-1589**. These wars came to an end when Henri of Navarre, a Huguenot leader, became King Henri IV of France. Henri succeeded in uniting the country by converting to Catholicism, while allowing toleration for the Huguenots with the Edict of Nantes (**1598**).

Henri IV

1560-1574 Reign of Charles IX of France.

1563 English Poor Law: Justices of the Peace are entitled to raise a poor rate to look after the poor in each parish.

1564-1616 Life of William Shakespeare, English playwright and poet.

The Globe Theatre, London, where Shakespeare's plays were performed

1567-1625 Reign of James VI of Scotland, later James I of England.

1572 St. Bartholomew's Day Massacre: 20,000 Huguenots are murdered by troops acting on behalf of the French regent, Queen Catherine de' Medici.

1574

Northern and Eastern Europe

1553-1555 Richard Chancellor, an English navigator, goes on expeditions to Russia.

1555 Peace of Augsburg: Emperor Charles V allows the Protestant princes freedom of worship.

1555 English Muscovy Company is given a charter to explore and trade with Russia.

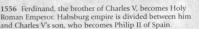

Muscovy Company coat-of-arms

1556 Ferdinand, the brother of Charles V, becomes Holy Roman Emperor. Habsburg empire is divided between him and Charles V's son, who becomes Philip II of Spain.

1557-1582 Russia, Poland, Sweden and Denmark fight over territories in the Baltic.

1563-1570 War between Sweden and Denmark, which ends with the Peace of Stettin. Livonia is partitioned between Poland and Denmark.

1564-1576 Reign of Maximilian II, Holy Roman Emperor.

THE DUTCH REVOLT

When Philip II of Spain inherited the Netherlands in **1555**, much of the population had already converted to Calvinism. So when Philip tried to impose Catholicism, he met with opposition. By **1566**, Calvinist worship had become public, and there were attacks on Catholic churches. In **1568**, the Spanish governor executed Calvinist counts, Hoorn and Egmont, and rebels, known as Sea Beggars, escaped to sea to attack Spanish ships. This marked the start of a long struggle, known as the Dutch Revolt. It finally came to an end when the Spanish recognized Dutch independence, at the Peace of the Hague in **1648**.

1571 Battle of Lepanto (off the Greek coast): Turks defeated by Spain and Venice. The end of Turkish sea power in Europe.

1571 Tartars (Mongols) from the Crimea destroy Moscow.

1572 Poland introduces a system of electing kings.

1572 Dutch Sea Beggars capture towns of Briel (Brill) and Vlissingen (Flushing) in the Netherlands.

1573 Henri of Valois (later Henri III of France) becomes the first elected King of Poland.

Africa and the Middle East

c.1550s England starts trading with West Africa.

1551 Ottoman Turks take Tripoli, Syria. War between Turkey and Hungary.

1554-1555 War between the Turks and the Persian Safavids.

Safavid warriors

1562 England joins the slave trade, shipping slaves from West Africa to the Caribbean. John Hawkins, a navigator, allies with two kings in Sierra Leone and attacks local tribes, taking captives as slaves.

Map showing the slave routes

1566 The Ottoman empire is now at its greatest extent.

1566-1574 Reign of Sultan Selim II of Turkey.

1573 Don John of Austria captures Tunis, North Africa and Turkey goes to war with Austria.

1574-1595 Reign of Sultan Murad III of Turkey.

1574 Portuguese colonize Angola.

1574-1575 Ottoman Turks retake Tunis and conquer the rest of Tunisia.

Ottoman ceramics

Asia

1550 The Mongol leader, Altan-Khan, invades northern China. Japanese pirates raid China.

1555 Humayun regains his Indian empire from Sher Shah.

1555 The King of Toungoo captures the northern Burmese kingdom of Ava. This results in a unified Burmese state, which grows at the expense of the Thai kingdom.

1556-1605 Reign of Akbar the Great, greatest of the Mogul rulers. A new phase of conquest begins.

Akbar (on the second elephant) pursuing his enemies

1556 Astrakhan is annexed by Russia.

1557 Portuguese establish a settlement at Macao. Trade with China is restricted to Macao.

1560 Oda Nobunaga becomes leading *daimyo* (landowner) in Japan.

1564 Spaniards occupy the Philippines and build Manila.

1565 Akbar extends the Mogul empire to the Deccan.

1567 Oda Nobunaga becomes *shogun* (military dictator) of Japan.

1570 Nagasaki, Japan, is opened to foreign traders. Traders come via Macao, China, bringing silk.

1573-1577 Akbar conquers Gujerat and Bengal and unifies northern India.

Japanese samurai helmet

Map of Japan

HOKKAIDO

HONSHU

Edo (Tokyo)

Hiroshima

Osaka

Nagasaki

KYUSHU

The Americas

1554 São Paulo, Brazil, is founded.

SOUTH AMERICA

São Paulo

Golden conure (left) and macaws from the Amazon rainforest in Brazil

c.1560 Silver from Mexico and Peru is established as the chief export from the Americas to Spain.

These Mexican gold bars were salvaged from a shipwreck.

1560 Titu Cusi Inca rules at Vilcabamba, Peru.

1562-1565 French colony in Florida is destroyed by the Spaniards.

1562 John Hawkins makes his first slave trade voyage to Hispaniola (Haiti). Second and third voyages follow: 1564-1565 and 1567-1568.

1572 Sir Francis Drake, an English navigator, attacks Spanish ports in America.

1572 Topa Amaru, the last Inca ruler, is captured and executed.

Inca soldiers like these were no match for the Spaniards.

Southern and Western Europe

1577-1580 Sir Francis Drake, English navigator, sails around the world.

A viol, used for early ballet music

1580-1640 Union of Spain and Portugal.

1581 First known ballet, *Le Ballet Comique de la Reine*, is performed at the marriage of the Queen of France's sister.

Dancing shoes were worn, as there were no special ballet shoes.

1582 Gregorian Calendar (the one we use today) is devised by Pope Gregory XIII, and introduced in Catholic countries.

1586 The War of the 3 Henries in France: Henri III, Henri of Guise and Henri of Navarre.

1587 Mary, Queen of Scots, is executed by Elizabeth I for plotting against her. Elizabeth accepts Mary's son, the Protestant James VI of Scotland, as her heir.

1588 The defeat of the Spanish Armada, a fleet of ships sent by Philip II to conquer England.

Gold found in the wreckage of the Spanish ship Girona, sunk off the Irish coast

Spanish galleons were huge and slow, more suited to defending than attacking.

1589 Henri III is murdered. The crown is claimed by Henri of Navarre as Henri IV of France, first king of the Bourbon dynasty.

1590 Henri IV defeats French Catholics at the Battle of Ivry.

1592 Presbyterianism (a form of Calvinism) is adopted in Scotland, influenced by the teachings of John Knox.

1593 Henri IV of France becomes a Catholic.

1594 Henri IV of France enters Paris and begins his reign.

1596 Galileo Galilei (**1564-1642**), an Italian astronomer, mathematician and physicist, invents the thermometer.

1596 English attack Cadiz, on the southwest coast of Spain, and upset the preparation of a second Armada.

1597 Irish rebellion against the English, led by Hugh O'Neill, Earl of Tyrone.

1598 Henri IV of France issues the Edict of Nantes, allowing religious toleration to Huguenots (French Protestants).

Northern and Eastern Europe

1576 Spanish soldiers sack Antwerp. Pacification of Ghent: 17 Netherlands provinces unite to drive out the Spaniards.

1576 Russia begins expanding across the Ural mountains.

1578 Peace of Arras: 10 southern provinces of the Netherlands unite with Spain.

1579 Union of Utrecht: the seven northern provinces of the Netherlands unite against Spain.

1581 Russians begin the conquest of Siberia.

Russian aristocrats known as boyars

1581 Seven northern provinces of the Netherlands proclaim independence as the United Provinces and elect William, Prince of Orange, as their ruler.

1582 Peace between Russia and Poland. Russia is cut off from the Baltic Sea.

1584 William of Orange, ruler of the United Provinces, is assassinated.

1585 Gerardus Mercator (**1512-1594**), a Flemish geographer and map-maker, introduces a more accurate way of drawing maps than had previously been used.

1587-1688 Catholic Vasa dynasty rules Poland.

1596 France, England and the United Provinces unite against Spain.

1598 Death of Tsar Theodor, last of the Rurik dynasty: the start of a period known as "the time of troubles" in Russia.

Early print of the city of Moscow

THE 16TH CENTURY 1575-1599

Africa and the Middle East

1578 King Sebastian of Portugal invades Morocco, but is defeated at the Battle of al-Ksar al-Kabir. Ahmed al Mansur of Fez establishes the Sharifian dynasty and Morocco expands in power.

1580 1617 Reign of Idris Alooma, greatest of the kings of the Kanem-Bornu.

1581 Moroccans begin penetrating the Sahara Desert.

Dromedary camel found in the Sahara

1581 Peace between Turkey and Spain.

1585 Ottoman empire begins to decline.

1586-1622 Reign of Shah Abbas the Great in Persia.

1590 Moroccans reach the Niger and take Timbuktu.

1590 Shah Abbas of Persia makes peace with Turkey.

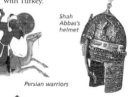

Shah Abbas's helmet

Persian warriors

1591 Battle of Tondibi: Moroccans invade and defeat Songhai and cause the kingdom to collapse.

1592 Portuguese capture Mombasa, on the East African coast.

1598 Dutch capture Mauritius.

1598 Shah Abbas makes Isfahan the capital of Persia.

Asia

1579 Portuguese trading station is established in Bengal, India.

1581 Akbar subdues Afghanistan, formally annexing it in **1585**.

1581 Russians conquer Siberia.

1582-1598 Toyotomi Hideyoshi succeeds as leader in Japan.

1584 Phra Narai creates an independent kingdom of Siam.

1587 Akbar takes Kashmir, northern India.

1591 First English voyage to the East Indies.

Hindu statue from Java, Indonesia, East Indies

1592 Annamese take Hanoi and unite North Vietnam.

1592 Akbar conquers Sind, India.

1593 Japanese leave Korea under pressure from the Chinese.

1594 English begin trading in India.

1594 Mogul emperor Akbar conquers Kandahar, India.

1595 Dutch start to establish colonies in the East Indies.

1597 Japanese invade Korea, but the Chinese help the Koreans to expel them.

1598 Death of Toyotomi Hideyoshi, ruler of Japan. He is succeeded by a child, and five regents compete for power.

Japanese building called a pagoda, often built next to Buddhist temples

1599 Mogul emperor Akbar begins to conquer the Deccan, India.

The Americas

1576-1577 Martin Frobisher, an English navigator, explores North Atlantic and discovers Baffin Island.

Frobisher met local people, the Inuits, paddling in one-manned canoes called kayaks.

1577 Humphrey Gilbert, an English navigator, is granted a patent to found colonies in North America.

1579 Sir Francis Drake claims New Albion (California) during his voyage around the world (1577-1580).

Sir Francis Drake

1583 Humphrey Gilbert establishes the first English colony in Newfoundland.

1584 Walter Raleigh, (English) discovers and annexes Virginia. He founds a colony in **1585**, but it is abandoned by settlers in **1586**. A second colony is set up in 1587-1591.

1585-1587 John Davis, English explorer, searches for a northwest passage to Asia and explores the Davis Strait.

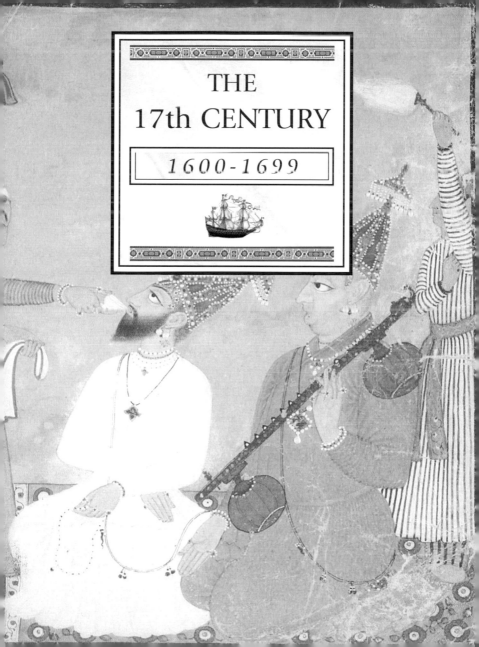

THE
17th CENTURY

1600-1699

Southern and Western Europe

1600 English East India Company is founded.

1602 Dutch East India Company is founded.

1603 Tudor dynasty ends with death of Elizabeth I. James VI of Scotland becomes James I of England and Scotland (1603-1625). The start of the Stuart dynasty.

Funeral procession for Elizabeth I

1604-1616 12 year truce in the Netherlands between the Spanish and the Dutch, supported by the English and French.

1605 Gunpowder Plot: a failed attempt by a group of English Catholics, including Guy Fawkes, to blow up the Houses of Parliament. They are caught and executed.

1605 Miguel Cervantes (1547-1616) writes *Don Quixote de la Mancha*, the first modern novel.

1608 The first practical telescope is invented by Hans Lippershey, a Dutch lens maker.

1609 Moors (North African Arabs) are expelled from Portugal.

1610 Galileo Galilei, an Italian astronomer and mathematician, publishes *The Starry Messenger*, about his discoveries with the use of a telescope.

1610 Assassination of Henri IV of France. Start of reign of Louis XIII (1610-1643).

1611 King James Bible published in England.

1614 John Napier, a Scottish mathematician, invents his logarithm tables.

1614-1616 Civil war in France.

1616 William Harvey, an English doctor, introduces the idea of the circulation of the blood around the body.

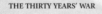

Two of Galileo's telescopes mounted on a stand

Northern and Eastern Europe

1603 Grigoriy Otrepieff, a monk, claims to be Dimitri, youngest son of the late Ivan IV, and heir to the Russian throne. (Dimitri had in fact been murdered in 1591.) Grigoriy invades Russia and is crowned Tsar, but becomes unpopular.

1604 Russians expand across Siberia and found Tomsk.

1606 Russia: the false Dimitri is defeated and murdered in a revolt led by Boris Gudunov.

1607-1611 Reign of Charles IX of Sweden.

1608 Formation of a Protestant Union in Germany.

1609 Maximilian of Bavaria forms a Catholic league.

1609 Johannes Kepler (1571-1630), a German astronomer, announces his laws of planetary motion. Kepler developed Copernicus's idea that planets revolve around the Sun, but suggested that they did so in ellipses rather than circles.

Tsarevich Dimitri (top) and Grigoriy Otrepieff, the false Dimitri (bottom)

Diagram of Kepler's idea of planetary motion

1611-1613 War between Sweden and Denmark.

1611-1632 Reign of Gustavus Adolphus II of Sweden, great soldier and statesman. Sweden acquires land on the Baltic and becomes a major power.

Gustavus Adolphus II

1613 Russia: Romanov dynasty (1613-1917) is founded by Tsar Michael.

1613 Turks conquer Hungary.

1617 Treaty of Stolbovo: Russia gives up Ingria and Karelia to Sweden.

THE THIRTY YEARS' WAR

The Thirty Years' War (1618-1648) began as a revolt by the Bohemian provinces of the Holy Roman Empire, but it soon merged with several other conflicts. Fought mainly in Germany, the war devastated the land, killing thousands. The two sides were divided mainly on religious lines, with Spain and Catholic German states supporting the Empire, and Denmark and Protestant German states supporting Bohemia. Later, political factors grew more important. In 1630, the Protestants were joined by Sweden, whose brilliant commander, Gustavus Adolphus, wanted to expand his own power in the Baltic. Catholic France, already at war with Spain, joined the Protestant side in 1635. The peace treaty in 1648 ended the threat of Habsburg domination.

The city of Magdeburg, Germany, under seige in 1631, from an early print

Africa to India

c.1600 Oyo kingdom in West Africa is at its height.

1602-1627 Wars between the Persian Safavids and the Ottoman Turks. Turks lose Baghdad (Iraq) in 1603, Tabriz (northwest Persia) in 1604 and Georgia in 1618.

1605 India: Emperor Akbar dies. Succeeded by Jahangir (1605-1627).

An Oyo carving

Jahangir, Mogul emperor

1609 Dutch take Ceylon from Portugal.

1610 English East India Company sets up a first factory in India at Madras.

1611 English East India Company establishes first trading post in India, at Surat.

1612 Persians take Baghdad (Iraq) from the Ottoman Turks.

The Blue Mosque, Isfahan, Persia

1616 Dutch and French establish trading posts in Senegal and the Gold Coast (Ghana), West Africa.

1616 English East India Company trades with Persia.

The Far East

c.1600 Dutch trading bases established in Java and Sumatra.

1600 Civil war in Burma: Burmese empire breaks up.

JAPAN UNDER THE TOKUGAWAS

In **1600**, Ieyasu Tokugawa won the Battle of Sekigahara, ending civil war, and in **1603** assumed the title of *shogun* (military ruler), founding

Ieyasu Tokugawa

the Tokugawa dynasty. The Tokugawa ruled Japan from their new capital, Edo (Tokyo), until 1867. They organized Japanese society into rigid classes, with *daimyo* (warlords) and *han* (fiefs) closely regulated by the shogun.

1602 First Dutch traders arrive in Cambodia and Siam.

Dutch tile

1605 Hidetada Tokugawa becomes ruler in Japan.

1606 Willem Jantszoon, Dutch navigator, is first European to reach Australia.

1613-1646 Reign of Sultan Agung of Mataram, who tries to rule Java.

1614-1636 Europeans begin to explore Australia.

1616 Manchu Tartars invade China.

1618-1629 Dutch expel Portuguese from East Indies. Set up base at Batavia (Jakarta), Sumatra in **1619**.

Puppets from Java, East Indies

The Americas

1602 Spaniards explore the coast of California.

1603 French start to colonize North America: Newfoundland, Nova Scotia and New France.

1605 Spaniards found Santa Fé, New Mexico.

1605 James I of England is proclaimed King of Barbados.

1606 First permanent English settlement in North America, at Jamestown, Virginia.

Early settlers

1608 French found Quebec, Canada.

1608 Paraguay founded by Jesuits.

1609 English settlers on Bermuda.

1609 Dutch found Manhattan.

1610-1611 Henry Hudson, English navigator, explores Hudson Bay, in search of northwest passage to East.

Native North Americans traded furs for guns, knives and blankets.

1610 Etienne Brulé, French explorer, discovers Lake Huron.

1612 Tobacco cultivated in Virginia.

1613 Samuel de Champlain, French explorer, explores Ottawa river, Canada.

1613 English destroy French settlement at Port Royal, Jamaica.

1616 Willem Schouten, Dutch navigator, rounds Cape Horn.

1619 First slaves imported into Virginia from West Africa.

1619 First colonial assembly is held at Jamestown, Virginia.

1600

1619

Southern and Western Europe

1620 Uprising of Huguenots (Protestants) in France.

1620s Johannes Kepler (1571-1630), a German astronomer, studies the movement of the planets.

1621-1625 Philip IV of Spain resumes war against the Dutch.

1622-1673 Life of Molière (born Jean-Baptiste Poquelin), great French comedy playwright.

1624-1629 France and England at war.

1624-1642 Cardinal Richelieu is first minister to Louis XIII of France.

1625-1649 Reign of Charles I of England.

1628 Cardinal Richelieu captures Huguenot stronghold of La Rochelle, ending Huguenot threat to French unity.

Cardinal Richelieu

Siege tower at La Rochelle, on the west coast of France

1629-1640 England: King Charles I dissolves Parliament after disagreements with the House of Commons over customs and excise duties and Catholicism. He does not recall Parliament until **1640**. Charles builds up his navy to rival that of the Dutch, levying an old tax called Ship Money to cover the cost.

Charles I

1632 Galileo Galilei (1564-1642), an Italian astronomer and mathematician, publishes his *Dialogues*, which revolutionizes scientific thinking.

Galileo's telescope and his sketches of the moon

1635 France declares war on Spain and joins the Thirty Years' War.

1637 René Descartes, French mathematician, does important work on analytical geometry.

Northern and Eastern Europe

1620 Battle of the White Mountain outside Prague: victory for the imperial forces in the Thirty Years' War.

1621 Gustavus Adolphus gains Livonia from Poland.

1622 England sends first ambassador to Turkey.

1623 Protestant worship is forbidden in Bohemia.

1625 Denmark joins the Thirty Years' War.

1628 Swedish royal flagship, the *Vasa*, sinks in Stockholm shortly after being launched.

The Vasa

1629 Peace of Lübeck between Denmark and the Holy Roman Empire.

1630 Sweden joins the Thirty Years' War.

1631 Battle of Breitenfeld: imperial forces are defeated.

1632 Battle of Lützen: Swedes defeat imperial forces, but King Gustavus Adolphus is killed.

1632 Russians continue to expand in Siberia: Irkutsk is founded.

Russian fur traders in Siberia, from an old print

1632-1654 Reign of Queen Christina of Sweden, guided by the great statesman, Axel Oxenstierna.

1634 Battle of Nördlingen: Sweden loses South Germany.

Map showing the growth of the Swedish empire

Sweden, 1560

Expansion to 1645

Expansion to 1658

Boundary 1658

RUSSIA

KINGDOM OF NORWAY AND DENMARK

SWEDISH KINGDOM

KARELIA

Narva · INGRIA

• Stockholm

ESTONIA

LIVONIA

HALLAND

GOTLAND

Kalmar

Baltic sea

Copenhagen

Roskilde • • Lund

POLISH KINGDOM

Africa to India

1627-1656 Rule of Mogul emperor, Shah Jahan, who adds territories to the empire. From 1632-1653, he builds the white marble Taj Mahal, a tomb for his beloved wife Mumtaz Mahal.

Shah Jahan and the Taj Mahal

1628 Portuguese destroy the Mwenemutapa kingdom in southern Africa.

1629 Death of Shah Abbas the Great of Persia.

1631-1642 Dutch West India Company ousts the Portuguese from the Gold Coast (Ghana).

1636 Sultans of the Deccan, India, become subject princes of the Moguls.

1637 Dutch take El Mina, West Africa, from the Portuguese.

1637 French establish trading posts in Senegal, West Africa.

1639 Ottoman Turks make peace with the Persians after capturing Iraq from them.

A Mogul sword

The Far East

1622-1624 Christian missionaries are executed in Japan.

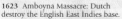

Japanese Samurai sword scabbard and sword guard

1623 Amboyna Massacre: Dutch destroy the English East Indies base.

1623-1651 Rule of the powerful shogun Iemitsu Tokugawa in Japan. Fearing foreign influence or invasion, he forbids all Japanese to travel abroad and almost all existing foreign merchants are expelled: only the Dutch are allowed to remain on the island of Nagasaki.

1626-1662 Dutch trade with China from Formosa (Taiwan).

1627 Manchu people from Manchuria, northern China, begin expanding into other parts of China and Korea.

1636 Manchus proclaim a new Chinese dynasty, the Ch'ing, at Mukden, Manchuria.

1637 Korea becomes a subject state of China.

1637 English establish a trading post in Canton, China.

1639-1850s Japan enforces isolationist policies. Japanese are forbidden to go abroad and foreigners banned from entering Japan. Japan becomes virtually isolated from European contact. During this period, towns grow and trade flourishes.

Manchu armies attacking

Illustration of wealthy Japanese woman

The Americas

1620 *The Mayflower* sails from Plymouth, England, to Massachusetts, carrying the Pilgrims (English Puritans).

Wild North American turkey

1625 French establish a port at Cayenne, Guiana.

Pilgrims at Thanksgiving meal

1625 Dutch found New Amsterdam (now New York).

1627 French Cardinal Richelieu sets up a company to colonize all land between Florida and the Arctic.

1629 English capture Quebec from France (restored to France 1632).

1630-1642 16,000 settlers join the Massachusetts Bay Colony.

1634 Maryland is founded for Catholic colonists.

1634 Dutch establish a base at Curaçao, West Indies.

1634 Jean Nicolet, French explorer, explores Lake Michigan and St. Lawrence and Mississippi rivers.

1636 Founding of Dutch Guiana (Becomes British Guiana in 1811).

1636-1637 Pequot War between settlers and native North Americans in New England.

Native American Indians from the East coast

1620

1639

Southern and Western Europe

1640 England: Charles I summons Parliament to raise money to fight the Scots.

1640 Portugal becomes independent under the house of Braganza (until **1910**).

1642 Blaise Pascal, a French mathematician, designs a mechanical adding machine.

THE ENGLISH CIVIL WAR

The English Civil War (**1642-1649**) was the result of a rift between Parliament and the early Stuart kings, James I (**1603-1625**), and Charles I (**1625-1649**). MPs felt the kings were claiming too much power, and attempting to rule without them. Many of them were Puritans (strict Protestants) and they suspected the kings of Catholic sympathies. War began in **1642**. By **1646**, the Roundheads (the Parliamentary side), led by Oliver Cromwell and his New Model Army, had defeated the Cavaliers (the King's side). Fighting broke out again between **1648-1649**, ending with the defeat and execution of Charles I.

Helmet

Charles I

1643 Evangelista Torricelli (**1608-1647**), a Florentine, invents the barometer.

1643 French beat the Spaniards at the Battle of Rocroi: the start of French military superiority in Europe.

1643-1715 Louis XIV of France comes to the throne, aged 5. His mother reigns for him until **1651**, and policy is controlled by first minister Cardinal Mazarin until **1661**.

1644 René Descartes, a French mathematician and philosopher, publishes his *Principles of Philosophy*.

1648 Peace of the Hague ends the Dutch Revolt. Spain recognizes independent United Provinces (Dutch Republic).

1648-1653 Riots in Paris: period of civil disorder in France known as the Fronde.

1649-1660 England is ruled by the Commonwealth (**1649-1653**), then the Protectorate (**1653-1658**), under Oliver Cromwell.

1649 Oliver Cromwell puts down Scottish and Irish rebellions.

1652-1654 First Anglo-Dutch Trade War.

c.1658 Robert Boyle, Irish scientist, and Robert Hooke, English scientist, design and build a new air pump to create a vacuum in a glass tube.

Hooke and Boyle's air pump

1659 Peace of the Pyrenees between France and Spain.

Northern and Eastern Europe

1640-1688 The state of Brandenburg-Prussia grows in importance under Frederick William, "the Great Elector".

Frederick William I

Map showing Brandenburg-Prussia 1648-1707

Map labels: EAST PRUSSIA, EAST POMERANIA, BRANDENBURG, Magdeburg, Berlin, Potsdam, Brandenburg in 1648, Land acquired 1648-1707

1643-1645 War between Sweden and Denmark. Sweden becomes the major power in the Baltic.

1645-1659 War between Venice and the Turks leads to the conquest of Crete by the Turks.

1646 Swedes take Prague and invade Bavaria.

1648 Peace of Westphalia ends the Thirty Years' War.

1649 The Code of Laws marks the establishment of serfdom in Russia. (Serfs are peasants with no land of their own.)

1649 Russians reach the Pacific Ocean and found Okhotsk in eastern Siberia.

Queen Christina of Sweden

1654 Queen Christina of Sweden abdicates and becomes a Catholic.

1654-1657 War between Russia and Poland. Russia acquires Smolensk and eastern Ukraine.

1654-1660 War between Sweden and Poland.

1657 Elector of Brandenburg wins the sovereignty of Prussia.

1658 Peace of Roskilde: the Danes give up all claims to southern Sweden.

Africa to India

1640 English acquire the port of Madras, India.

1643 French establish Fort Dauphin, Madagascar.

1644 Dutch settle in Mauritius.

1648 Arabs recapture Muscat from Portugal.

1650 Ali Bey makes himself hereditary governor of Tunis, North Africa.

1651 English occupy St. Helena, in the Atlantic Ocean.

1652 Dutch found the Cape of Good Hope, South Africa.

Cape Dutch farmhouse

1656-1661 Grand Vizier Mohammed Köprülü saves the Ottoman empire from decline.

1656 Dutch displace the Portuguese in Ceylon (Sri Lanka).

1656-1707 Rule of Aurangzeb, the last great Mogul emperor. He defeats and deposes his father, Jahan, and conquers Kandahar, Kabul and the Deccan. The empire reaches its greatest extent, but decay sets in.

Peacock kept at Emperor's palace

Elephants dressed for Mogul celebration

1659 French found trading posts on coast of Senegal.

The Far East

1641 Dutch seize Malacca from Portugal and dominate trade in East Indies.

1641 Japan cuts itself off from the rest of the world. Dutch keep a trading post on an island off Nagasaki.

Nagasaki Bay

1642 Abel Tasman, Dutch explorer, discovers Van Diemen's Land (Tasmania) and New Zealand.

1643 Tasman discovers Fiji islands.

1644 Abel Tasman explores the north and west coasts of Australia.

THE CH'ING DYNASTY

In **1627**, the Manchu people began expanding into other parts of China, from their base at Mukden, Manchuria in northern China. In **1636**, they proclaimed a new Chinese dynasty, the Ch'ing. Meanwhile, rebellions broke out against the Chinese Ming dynasty. In **1644**, bandits occupied Beijing and the dynasty was deposed. The Chinese people then invited the Manchus to overthrow the bandits. By **1652** most of the country was under Ch'ing control. They ruled China from Beijing until 1911/1912.

The boundaries of China under the Ming and Ch'ing dynasties

1648 Bering Strait is discovered by Russian Cossack explorer, Dezhnev.

The Americas

1642 French found Montreal, Canada.

The Canadian fur trade continues to grow. These are some of the animals hunted for their fur.

Stoat

Beaver

Otter

Inuit bow

1643 New Hampshire is founded.

1644 Rhode Island separates from the Massachusetts Bay Colony.

1648 French establish settlements in the Caribbean islands of St. Martin, St. Bartholomew, St. Croix, The Saints, Maria Galante, St. Lucia and Grenada.

1648-1653 War between the Iroquois and the Huron and Algonquin tribes in North America.

c.1650 Settler population in the 13 North American colonies reaches about 60,000.

1651 Maine becomes part of the Massachusetts Bay Colony.

1654 First sugar cane plantations set up in the Caribbean by the English and French. Slaves are imported from West Africa to work on them.

1655 England acquires Jamaica from Spain.

1655 French acquire Haiti.

Southern and Western Europe

1660 The Restoration: Charles II is restored to the English throne.

LOUIS XIV - THE SUN KING

In **1661**, at the age of 22, Louis XIV took control of the government in France. During his reign, France became the dominant power in Europe, and literature, art, drama and music flourished at his court. In a series of brilliant military victories, he extended France's boundaries, provoking hostility and fear abroad. Under his minister, Colbert

Louis XIV

(1619-1683), the economy was modernized and Louis was able to control his nobles, ruling with absolute power. His absolutism - the idea that the power of the state should be embodied in one person (the monarch), who does not have to answer to anyone - became the model for other European rulers.

Louis XIV was nicknamed the "Sun King". This image is taken from his palace at Versailles.

1661 Robert Boyle, Irish scientist, defines chemical elements.

1664 French East India Company is founded.

1665-1667 Second Anglo-Dutch Trade War ends in the Peace of Breda.

1665 Portugal wins independence from Spain, with English help. Recognized at the Treaty of Lisbon (**1668**).

1665 Isaac Newton (1642-1727), English scientist, discovers gravity.

1665 The Great Plague in London.

The Fire of London

1666 The Great Fire of London.

1668 Isaac Newton invents the reflecting telescope.

1670 Treaty of Dover: a secret treaty between Charles II and Louis XIV, supplying Charles with funds to fight the Dutch and restore Catholicism in England.

1672-1674 Third Anglo-Dutch Trade War.

1672-1678 War between France and Netherlands ends in the Peace of Nijmegen.

1672-1702 William III of Orange is hereditary *stadtholder* (ruler) of the Netherlands.

1679 Exclusion Crisis in England: parliamentary bill prevents James, the Catholic Duke of York, from succeeding his brother as King of England. Charles II dismisses Parliament.

Northern and Eastern Europe

1660 Treaty of Oliva ends war between Sweden, Poland, Brandenburg and the Holy Roman Empire.

1660 Brandenburg acquires sovereignty over Prussia.

Prussian foot soldier

1660-1697 Reign of Charles XI of Sweden.

1661 First European banknote is issued by the Bank of Stockholm, Sweden.

1663-1699 Ottoman Turks attack Central Europe.

1664 Ottoman Turks invade and occupy Hungary.

1667 End of a 13-year truce between Russia and Poland. Kiev is ceded to Russia.

Early Swedish banknote

1669 Venice cedes Crete to the Turks, marking the end of Venice's colonial empire.

1670 Rebellion of Ukrainian Cossacks and peasants subject to Poland is crushed by the Polish leader, Jan Sobieski.

1671 Turks declare war on Poland, in support of Cossacks.

1672 Turks and Cossacks invade Poland. Poles give up Podolia and Ukraine.

Cossack soldiers dancing

1673 Poles defeat the Turks at the Battle of Khorzim.

1674 Jan Sobieski is elected King of Poland.

1675 Elector of Brandenburg defeats the Swedes at the Battle of Fehrbellin.

1676 Peace of Zuravno ends the war between Poland and Turkey. Turkey gains the Polish Ukraine.

1676 Swedes defeat the Danes at the Battle of Lund.

1677 Swedes defeat Danes at Rostock and Landström.

1677-1979 War between Russia and Turkey. At the Treaty of Radzin, Russia gains most of Ukraine from Turks.

1678 War between Russia and Sweden.

1679 Peace between Sweden and Brandenburg.

Africa to India

c.1660-1670 Rise of the Bambara kingdoms of the Upper Niger, West Africa.

1662 Battle of Ambuila: Portuguese destroy the Kongo kingdom, Central Africa.

Carving from the Kongo kingdom

1662 Portuguese cede Tangier, North Africa to England.

1666-1668 Civil wars in India.

1668 English East India Company obtains control of Bombay, India.

1669 Aurangzeb bans Hinduism in India and persecutes Hindus.

1672 English Royal Africa Company merges with the Guinea Company. West African trade increases.

1674 French establish a trading station at Pondicherry, India.

1674 Sivaji Bhonsla, leader of the Marathas, breaks away from Moguls and founds a Maratha state in India.

1676 Uprising of Sikhs, a reformed Hindu sect, in India.

The Sikh Golden Temple, Amritsar, rebuilt in 1766 after attacks by the Moguls

The Far East

1661 Two Jesuit priests, John Grueber and Albert d'Orville, travel from Beijing, China to Agra, India and become the first Europeans to visit the city of Lhasa, in Tibet.

The Palace of Potala at Lhasa in Tibet, the residence of the dalai lamas, the political and religious rulers of Tibet

1661-1688 Rule of King Narai of Siam. He tries to resist Dutch attempts to monopolize trade by enlisting French help. This proves unpopular and his dynasty is overthrown, and the French soldiers expelled.

1662-1722 Reign of the powerful Chinese emperor, K'ang Hsi.

K'ang Hsi, Emperor of China

1663 French missionaries enter Vietnam.

1667 Dutch increase their territory in Java.

1679 War between Vietnam and Cambodia. Cambodia loses the Mekong river delta.

The Americas

1663 European settlers in the Carolinas.

1665 England gains New Netherlands (New York and New Jersey) and Caribbean islands from the Dutch.

1670 Hudson's Bay Company is founded in England to explore and acquire territory in the Hudson Bay area of Canada. They claim the fur trading area of Rupert's Land.

1673 Jacques Marquette and Louis Jolliet, French explorers, reach the headwaters of the Mississippi river.

1674 Plantations in Quebec, Canada, become French royal colonies.

1675-1676 War between settlers and Native Americans in New England. Settlers win control of the North American seaboard.

1679 Robert de la Salle, French explorer, explores the Great Lakes.

Map of the Great Lakes

Lake Superior

Lake Huron

Lake Ontario

Niagara Falls, explored by de la Salle

Lake Michigan

Lake Erie

Niagara Falls

Southern and Western Europe

1685 The revocation of the Edict of Nantes forces half a million Huguenots to flee France.

1685 Catholic James II becomes King of England. A Protestant uprising on behalf of Charles's illegitimate son, the Duke of Monmouth, is defeated.

1686 League of Augsburg: Holy Roman Empire, Spain, Sweden, Saxony, Bavaria and the Palatinate ally against France.

1687 Isaac Newton publishes the *Principia*, containing his three Laws of Motion and theory of gravitation.

Pages from Newton's book, the Principia

A device designed to demonstrate Newton's Third Law of Motion

1688-1689 Glorious Revolution in England: The House of Lords invites William of Orange to save England from Catholicism. James II flees to France. William becomes King of England and reigns with his wife Mary (daughter of James II) as William III and Mary II (**1689-1702**).

William III of Orange and his wife Mary II of England

1688-1697 War of the League of Augsburg.

1689 Parliament confirms the abdication of James II. Declaration of Rights safeguards Parliament and bars Catholics from throne.

1690 Battle of the Boyne: Irish Catholic supporters of the exiled James II are defeated by English forces.

1692 Scotland: massacre at Glencoe of members of the MacDonald clan (supporters of the Catholic James II) by the Campbells (supporters of the Protestant English throne).

1694-1778 Life of Voltaire, French writer and philosopher, author of *Candide*.

1697 Treaty of Rijswick ends the War of the League of Augsburg. France recognizes William III as the King of England and the Protestant succession of Queen Anne.

1698 England, France, United Provinces and HRE agree on the Spanish succession. Charles II of Spain makes a will, leaving his possessions to the Elector Prince of Bavaria.

1699 The Elector of Bavaria dies.

Northern and Eastern Europe

1682 Sighting of Great Comet (named Halley's Comet) by Edmund Halley. The comet had also appeared in **1066**, before the Battle of Hastings, and in **1531** and **1607**.

Halley's Comet shown in the Bayeux tapestry, made after the Battle of Hastings

1682 Princess Sophia becomes regent of Russia, on the accession of the 10-year-old Peter (see below).

1683 Ottomans besiege Vienna for the last time and fail. Turkish threat in Europe declines and Austrian power grows.

1684 The Holy League (Holy Roman Empire, Poland and Venice) is formed by Pope Innocent XI to fight the Turks.

1687 Battle of Mohacs: Turks are defeated and Hungary becomes a hereditary Habsburg possession.

PETER THE GREAT

Peter the Great (**1689-1725**) was one of the greatest rulers in Russian history. Coming to the throne in **1682**, at the age of 10, Peter took sole control in **1689** when he was just 17. Under his leadership, Russia developed into a major European power. Peter founded the Russian navy, strengthened the army and extended Russia's boundaries. To give himself a "window on the west", he built a new capital city, St. Petersburg, on the Baltic Sea. Peter's reforms strengthened and modernized the country: he improved education and introduced new industries and crafts. But, despite this, most people continued to live as serfs (landless peasants) and benefited little from Russia's development.

Peter the Great

The Winter Palace at St. Petersburg

1690 Turks take Belgrade, Serbia, in a counterattack against the Austrian empire.

1691 War continues between Turks and Austrians. Turks are defeated at Zelankemen. Habsburgs conquer Transylvania.

1695-1706 Russo-Turkish War: Russia captures Azov, a fort on the Black Sea, and Kamchatka, a peninsula at the eastern end of the continent.

1697 Battle of Zenta, Serbia: Prince Eugene of Savoy defeats the Turks.

1699 Treaty of Karlowitz: the Austrians recover Hungary, Croatia and Transylvania from the Turks. Poland takes the Turkish Ukraine. Venice gains Peloponnese and Podolia.

Africa to India

1680 Death of Sivaji Bhonsla, great leader of the Hindu Marathas in India.

Sivaji Bhonsla

1680-1708 French increase their trading activities in Madagascar and Nigeria.

1681 India: Prince Akbar leads an unsuccessful revolt against his father, Aurangzeb, and flees to the Deccan.

1686 Madagascar is annexed by the French East India Company.

1687 English East India Company transfers its headquarters from Surat to Bombay.

c.1690 Mogul empire reaches its greatest extent.

1690 English establish a trading base in Calcutta, India.

Kabul
Kandahar
Amritsar
Delhi
INDIA
Surat
Calcutta
Bombay
DECCAN
Madras
Pondicherry
CEYLON

Mogul empire in c.1690
Maratha territories in 1680

Map of India

1697-1712 Expansion of the Ashanti kingdom in West Africa.

The Ashanti were famous for their carving in gold.

The Far East

1680 Dutch territories in the East Indies are joined together.

1683 Manchus conquer Formosa (Taiwan).

1683 Dutch traders are admitted to Canton, China.

1684 Dutch take control in Java.

1685 Chinese ports are opened to foreign trade.

Chinese woodcut of a flat-bottomed boat, called a junk

1688 King Narai of Siam dies. Siamese policies become isolationist until the 1850s.

King Narai on an elephant

1688 William Dampier, English adventurer, explores Australia.

1697 Chinese conquer western Mongolia.

1698 First French legation to China.

1699 Dampier leads expedition to the Pacific, increasing European knowledge of the South Seas.

William Dampier, who may have been the inspiration for Daniel Defoe's novel, Robinson Crusoe.

The Americas

1680 Portuguese establish the colony of Sacramento, Uruguay.

1681 William Penn, an English Quaker, is granted a charter to found colony of Pennsylvania.

1682 Robert de la Salle, French explorer founds St. Louis and takes the Mississippi Valley.

De la Salle exploring the Mississippi river

1683 William Penn founds Philadelphia and Quaker colony of Pennsylvania. Penn makes a treaty with the Native Americans, which keeps Pennsylvania at peace.

Native North Americans often smoked a peace pipe, like this one, after peace was made.

1684 Bermuda becomes an English Crown Colony.

1688 German Quakers make first anti-slavery protests in North America.

1691 Massachusetts absorbs the Plymouth colony.

1691 The Carolinas are divided into North and South.

1691 English found Kingston, Jamaica.

1699 French found Louisiana.

Early settlers and explorers were often powerless when attacked by bears.

1680

1699

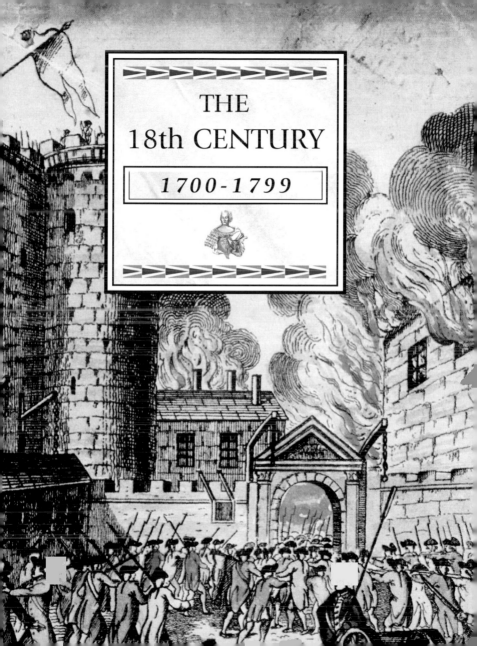

THE
18th CENTURY

1700-1799

Southern and Western Europe

WAR OF THE SPANISH SUCCESSION

Shields of claimants to the throne

The War of the Spanish Succession (**1701-1714**) was fought by major European countries to determine who would inherit the kingdom of the childless Charles II of Spain. With land in Italy and the Spanish Netherlands, and rich colonies in America, it was a valuable prize. There were claims both by the French Bourbons and the Austrian Habsburgs: Philip, grandson of Louis XIV of France, and Charles, son of Emperor Leopold, both claimed the throne. Fearing French supremacy, the English and Dutch formed an alliance to support Austria, later joined by Portugal and Savoy, and they won a series of brilliant victories. But in **1711**, Charles became emperor, altering the balance of power, and the English and Dutch swapped sides to support Philip. In the Peace of Utrecht (**1713-1714**), Philip became Philip V of Spain, but on the condition that Spain and France should never unite.

1702-1714 Reign of Queen Anne, the last of the Stuart monarchs of England.

1704 England seizes Gibraltar from Spain.

1704 Battle of Blenheim: Anglo-Austrians, led by the Duke of Marlborough and Prince Eugene of Savoy, save Vienna from French and Bavarians.

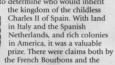

The Duke of Marlborough

1706 Thomas Newcomen, an English engineer, invents the first practical working steam engine for use in coal mining.

Union Jack

1707 Union of England and Scotland. The British Isles become known as Great Britain.

1709 Bartolomeo Cristofori (Italian) builds the first piano.

1710 St. Paul's Cathedral in London is completed.

St. Paul's Cathedral

1712-1778 Life of Jean-Jacques Rousseau, French writer and philosopher.

1714-1727 Reign of George I of Great Britain, first king of the German house of Hanover.

1715 Uprising in Scotland by Jacobites, supporters of James Edward, son of James II and pretender to the throne.

1718 Quadruple alliance is formed by Austria, Britain, France and Netherlands against Spain.

Northern and Eastern Europe

c.1700 Great age of Baroque music in Europe: J.S.Bach (**1685-1750**), Handel (**1685-1759**) and Vivaldi (**1675-1741**).

A violin, a popular Baroque instrument

For the orchestra 1750

Violin	12	Oboes	2	
Viola	6	Strings Bassoon	2	Wind
Cello	6	Horn	2	
Double Bass	6			
Harpsichord 1 or 2 } Continuo				

Also available – Trumpets and drums for festive occasions
Recorders for French and Venetian Opera
Trombones for Church music.

List of instruments in a Baroque orchestra

1700-1721 Great Northern War: a struggle for supremacy in the Baltic between Russia and Sweden. Swedes defeat Russians at Narva (**1700**) and invade Poland (**1701-1702**).

1701 Elector Frederick III of Brandenburg crowns himself Frederick I, "King in Prussia" (**1701-1713**).

1703 Peter the Great of Russia founds St. Petersburg.

An engraving of St. Petersburg

1703-1711 Hungarians revolt against Austria.

1706 Treaty of Altranstadt: Augustus II renounces the Polish throne and is replaced by Stanislaus Leszczynski.

1708-1709 Charles XII of Sweden invades Russia and is defeated at the Battle of Poltava (**1709**).

1709 Augustus II regains the Polish throne.

1710-1711 War between Russia and Turkey.

1710 Russia conquers Swedish Baltic provinces.

1712 St. Petersburg becomes capital of Russia.

1713-1740 Reign of Frederick William I of Prussia: Prussia develops as a strong military state.

1716-1718 War between Turkey and Austria ends with Peace of Passarowitz: Turkey cedes Belgrade to Austria and Hungary is liberated from Austria.

1718 Gabriel Fahrenheit, German scientist, invents the mercury thermometer.

1719 Russians invade Sweden. A coalition of Denmark, Sweden, Prussia and Britain is formed to oppose Russia.

Africa to India

c.1700 West Africa: kingdoms of Ashanti, Benin and Oyo flourish. The Ashanti are known for their work in gold. Yoruba kingdom declines.

Ashanti leather and brass shield

Gold cockerel

c.1700 East Africa: rise of the Bantu kingdom of Buganda.

c.1700 Oman controls Zanzibar and extends its influence along the East African coast. Portuguese influence declines.

1705 Turkish rule is overthrown in Tunis and Hussain Ibn Ali establishes the Hussainid dynasty.

1707 Mogul empire disintegrates after the death of Aurangzeb.

1708 English East India Company territories in India are divided between Bengal, Madras and Bombay.

1708 Revolution in Ethiopia.

1709-1711 Afghans rise against their Persian overlords and set up an independent Afghan state.

1711 Tripoli, Syria, becomes independent from Turkey.

1712-1755 Bambara kingdoms grow in the Upper Niger, West Africa.

1714 Ahmed Bey sets up Karamanli dynasty in Tripoli, Syria.

1714-1720 Hindu Maratha princes from central India increase their territory in northern India.

1715 French take control in Mauritius.

Maratha soldier

The Far East

1700 English East India Company establishes a base in Borneo.

1700 William Dampier, English navigator, discovers the north coast of New Guinea.

1707 Last eruption of Mount Fujiyama in Japan.

1714-1733 Reign of King Taninganway Min of Burma. Flourishing period of Burmese culture and power.

1715 China conquers Mongolia and East Turkestan.

1715 English East India Company builds its first factory at Canton, China.

Port of Canton in the 18th century

1716 Emperor K'ang Hsi prohibits the teaching of Christianity in China.

1716-1745 Rule of Shogun Yoshimune of Japan.

1717 Bugis people from Selangor, Malaya, extend their influence in Johore.

America and the Pacific

1701 French set up base at Detroit to control the trade in Illinois.

1701 Yale College is founded in New Haven, Connecticut.

1701 Peace treaty between French and Native Americans in New France (Canada).

Stick and ball used in lacrosse, a game played by Native Americans

1703 Delaware becomes a colony.

1704 Deerfield, Massachusetts: massacre of British colonists by French and Native North Americans.

1709 First German settlers arrive in North America.

1713 Britain acquires Nova Scotia, Hudson Bay and Newfoundland from France.

1714-1716 War between French and Native Americans in New France.

1718 French found New Orleans.

THE SLAVE TRADE

From the early 18th century until the early 19th century, millions of slaves were shipped from West Africa to work on sugar and cotton plantations in America and the Caribbean. Conditions on board ship were cramped, unhealthy and hot, and more than a million died en route.

Diagram showing the cramped conditions of slaves on board ship

Head of cotton

Southern and Western Europe

1720 South Sea Bubble: South Sea Company fails in Britain, causing financial panic.

1720 John Law's Mississippi Company collapses in France. This leads to national bankruptcy.

1721-1742 Robert Walpole becomes the first Prime Minister of Great Britain.

Robert Walpole

1725 Treaty of Vienna between Philip V of Spain and Charles VI of Austria. Philip guarantees the Pragmatic Sanction, allowing the succession of Charles VI's daughter, Maria Theresa.

1726 Russia allies with Austria.

1727-1729 War between Spain and Britain over Gibraltar.

c.1730 Rococo, a highly decorative style applied to architecture and interiors, often including scrolls and shells, reaches the height of its popularity.

Examples of Rococo furniture and ornaments

1733 Pact between French and Spanish Bourbons.

1733 John Kay, British inventor, invents the flying shuttle loom, which improves weaving.

1734 France invades Lorraine.

1734 Spain takes the kingdom of Naples.

1737 Death of the Grand Duke of Tuscany marks the end of the rule of the Medici in Florence.

1739 John and Charles Wesley found the Methodist movement in Oxford, England. John travels all over the country preaching, especially to the poor.

1739 War of Jenkins' Ear between Britain and Spain, named after a Captain Jenkins who claimed that Spaniards had boarded his ship and cut off his ear.

Centurion, a British battleship used in the war against Spain

Northern and Eastern Europe

1720 Treaty of Stockholm between Sweden, Prussia, Hanover, Denmark, Savoy and Poland.

1721 Peace of Nystadt ends war between Russia and Sweden. Russia makes great gains (Estonia, Livonia and part of Karelia) and ends Swedish domination of the Baltic. Peter the Great is proclaimed Emperor of all the Russias.

Dragoon officer in Peter's army

1722-1723 War between Russia and Turkey. Russia makes gains on the Caspian Sea.

1725 Treaty of Hanover: alliance between Britain, France, Prussia, Sweden, Denmark and the Netherlands.

1725-1727 Empress Catherine I rules Russia, after the death of her husband, Peter the Great.

Catherine I of Russia

1732 Frederick William I of Prussia introduces military and administrative reforms.

1733 Death of Augustus II, Elector of Saxony and King of Poland.

1733-1738 War of the Polish Succession. France and Sweden support Stanislaus Leszczynski. Austria and Russia support Augustus II's son. Treaty of Vienna ends the war and Augustus III succeeds to the throne.

1735-1739 War between Russia and Turkey. Russia obtains the Black Sea port of Azov, so expanding Russian territory as far as the Black Sea.

SWEDEN

KARELIA

RUSSIA

Nystadt

St.Petersburg

Narva

Baltic Sea

LIVONIA

ESTONIA

Kiev •

• Moscow

• Poltava

Caspian Sea

Russia in 1689

Expansion 1689 - 1725 (under Peter)

Expansion by the end of the 18th century

Map showing the expansion of Russian territory

Africa to India

1721 French annex Mauritius.

1722-1730 Afghans invade Persia, bringing an end to Safavid rule. The Afghans are expelled in 1730.

1723 British Africa Company acquires land in Gambia.

1724 Hyderabad, India, wins independence from the Moguls.

1727 Morocco: death of ruler Mulai Ismail is followed by a period of anarchy.

1729 Portugal loses Mombasa to the Arabs.

1731-1743 West Africa: war between Kano and Bornu. Sultan of Bornu becomes overlord of Kano.

Bornu horsemen

1735 French East India Company sets up sugar industry on Mauritius.

Sugar cane

1736-1747 Nadir Khan rules Persia.

1737 Marathas extend their power in northern India.

1737-1739 Nadir Khan of Persia occupies northern and western India and Afghanistan and attacks Delhi. He takes Mogul Emperor Jahan's peacock throne back to Persia.

1739 Anglo-Maratha Treaty allows the British to trade in the Deccan.

The Far East

1720 China conquers Tibet.

Pandas, native to northwest China and Tibet

1721 China suppresses a revolt in Formosa (Taiwan).

1726 France establishes a settlement on the Seychelle Islands.

1727 Treaty between Russia and China settles borders.

THE CHINA TRADE

In the 17th and 18th centuries, China had a flourishing export trade through the port of Canton, exporting tea, silk, porcelain and crafts to Europe. Chinese style became increasingly fashionable in Europe, although the Chinese had no interest in western goods and asked to be paid only in silver. From 1736-1796, China was ruled by the powerful emperor, Ch'ien Lung. During his reign, the country prospered and the population increased. But there was increasing hostility to European missionaries and to imports of opium from India. This provoked tensions and led to the outbreak of the Opium Wars (see page 81).

Tea, Silk and Jade were some of China's main exports to Europe

America and the Pacific

1721-1722 Jacob Roggeveen, Dutch explorer, discovers Pacific islands of Samoa, Solomons and Easter Island.

Statues on Easter Island

1726 Spanish first settle in Montevideo, Uruguay.

1727 Coffee is planted in Brazil.

1727 Quakers demand the abolition of slavery.

1728 Vitus Bering, a Danish navigator, discovers the Bering Straits between Russia and America.

Detail of the map drawn by Bering

1729 North and South Carolina become British crown colonies.

1730 First sugar cane refinery is established in New York. The success of sugar cane plantations in the Caribbean, worked by slaves imported from Africa, leads to the expansion of the trade in sugar.

1733 Georgia, the last of the 13 Colonies, is founded.

1737 Richmond, Virginia, is founded.

Sugar plantation

Southern and Western Europe

MARIA THERESA

In **1740**, Maria Theresa became Archduchess of Austria and Queen of Bohemia and Hungary on the death of her father, Charles VI. Although the empire she inherited was decaying and bankrupt, and her land and titles were coveted by other countries, she emerged as one of the greatest rulers in modern history. She successfully fought the War of Austrian Succession (**1740-1748**) and the Seven Years' War (**1756-1763**) and built Austria into a strong, stable power. During her long reign, Vienna became one of the cultural capitals of Europe: painting, music and architecture thrived and great palaces were built. Among the musicians who played at her court was the six-year-old Wolfgang Amadeus Mozart.

Maria Theresa

1744 War between France and Britain in Europe, India and the West Indies. Lasts intermittently until 1815.

1744 Sighting of the most-tailed comet on record, the De Cheseaux comet. It had at least six bright tails.

1745 Second Jacobite uprising in Scotland attempts to put Charles Edward Stewart (Bonnie Prince Charlie) on the throne. English defeat the Jacobites at Culloden (1746).

Bonnie Prince Charlie

1746 France seizes the Austrian Netherlands (Belgium). They are restored to Austria in **1748**.

1748 Georges de Buffon, French naturalist, publishes 36 volume survey of natural history. He suggests fossils provide evidence of extinct species.

1748 Peace of Aix-la-Chapelle ends War of the Austrian Succession.

1750-1777 Reign of José I of Portugal. The chief minister, the Marquis of Pombal, is virtual military dictator from **1775**.

1751-1776 Denis Diderot compiles the *Encyclopedie*, which aims to record the total stock of knowledge of the time.

1755 Corsicans rise against Genoese rule.

1755 Publication of Samuel Johnson's dictionary.

1755 Earthquake destroys Lisbon, Portugal.

1756 Joseph Black, Scottish chemist, produces carbon dioxide by heating chemicals.

1756-1763 Seven Years' War caused by rivalry between Austria and Prussia in Europe, and Britain and France in America. Austria allies with France; and Britain with Prussia. Spain joins the Franco-Austrian alliance in **1759**.

French navy commander

Northern and Eastern Europe

Frederick's crown

FREDERICK THE GREAT

Frederick II of Prussia (**1740-1786**), known as Frederick the Great, was a brilliant soldier and statesman. By **1772**, he had merged Prussia's territories together, making Prussia the strongest German state after Austria. Frederick was also a keen musician, interested in the ideas of the Enlightenment. Although he was an "absolute" ruler (keeping power firmly in his own hands), he tried to modernize the country, and to provide strong but efficient government in the interests of the people. He promoted education, agriculture and industry, brought in a fairer legal system, abolished torture and censorship, and declared religious freedom.

Prussian soldier

1740 Frederick II of Prussia invades Silesia.

1741 Ivan VI of Russia is deposed and replaced by Empress Elizabeth (**1741-1762**), Peter the Great's daughter. German influence and the power of the nobles increase.

1741 French, Bavarian and Saxon troops occupy Prague. Charles Albert of Bavaria is recognized as King of Bohemia.

1742 Anders Celsius, Swedish scientist, invents the centigrade thermometer.

1744 Frederick II of Prussia invades Bohemia, but is repelled by Austrians and Saxons.

1745 Ewald von Kleist, German priest, invents the Leiden jar, an instrument that stores electricity.

The Leiden jar

1746 Russia and Austria ally against Prussia.

1747 Sweden allies with Prussia. Russia allies with Britain.

1749-1832 Life of Johann Wolfgang von Goethe, German poet, novelist and playwright.

1753 Carl von Linné, also known as Linnaeus, a Swedish botanist, publishes his system for classifying plants, the starting point for the modern classification of species.

A page from Linnaeus's Systema Naturae

1757 Russia joins the Franco-Austrian alliance and invades East Prussia. Prussian victory at Rossbach and Leuthen.

1759-1805 Life of Johann Christoph Friedrich von Schiller, German poet, playwright and historian.

Africa to India

c.1740 Lunda kingdom of Kazembe is established in Central Africa.

1740-1756 Bengal becomes independent of the Mogul empire.

Bengal tiger

1746 French take Madras from the British.

1746 East Africa: Mazrui dynasty in Mombasa becomes independent of Oman.

1747-1748 West Africa: Yoruba conquer Dahomey, Benin.

1748 British retake Madras: start of intense Anglo-French rivalry in India.

1751 Robert Clive, young clerk in the East India Company, defeats the French at Arcot: the end of French influence in Madras.

1756 Black Hole of Calcutta: Nawab of Bengal puts 146 British people into a tiny prison and many die.

Shah Alam, Nawab of Bengal

1757 Clive captures Calcutta and defeats the Nawab of Bengal at Plassey: the start of British supremacy in India.

Indian ivory chess pieces in form of British and Indian soldiers

1758 Marathas seize the Punjab and take Lahore.

The Far East

1743 Mataram, Java becomes a Dutch subject state.

1751-1759 China overruns Tibet, Dzungaria and the Tarim Basin.

1752 Mons people conquer Upper Burma. Burmese leader, Alaungpaya, rebels and proclaims himself king. He gains control of most of Upper Burma.

1753 Alaungpaya takes the capital, Ava, and the Shan states.

1755 Alaungpaya seizes Dagon (renamed Rangoon) from the Mons in Lower Burma.

Map of Southeast Asia

1755 Dutch East India Company holds supremacy in Java after war with Javanese Mataram kingdom.

Dutch East India Company ships

1756 Alaungpaya takes Pegu and now controls all Burma. His dynasty rules until 1885.

1757-1843 China reduces European influence by restricting foreign trade to Canton.

1758 Bugis people of Johore recognize Dutch tin trade monopoly.

1758-1759 China conquers East Turkestan.

America and the Pacific

1742 Russians explore Alaska.

1742 Venezuela becomes a separate province inside the Spanish South American empire.

1744-1748 King George's War, between Britain and France in North America.

1745 Vitus Bering, Danish navigator, discovers the Aleutian Islands.

Arctic tern, found in Alaska

1745 Canada: British capture French fortress of Louisbourg.

1748 British return Louisbourg to France, as a part of the peace settlement in Europe.

1750 Boundary commission fails to settle British-French boundary disputes in North America.

1752 Marquis Duquesne is appointed governor of Quebec.

1752 Benjamin Franklin, a publisher and politician from Boston, Massachusetts, shows that lightning is caused by electricity.

Benjamin Franklin

1754 French and Native Americans fight against the British in North America.

1759 British troops, led by General Wolfe, capture Quebec from France.

General Wolfe

Southern and Western Europe

1761 Spain invades Portugal for refusing to close its ports to British ships.

1762 Britain declares war on Spain.

1763 Peace of Paris ends the Seven Years' War.

THE INDUSTRIAL REVOLUTION

In the early 18th century, Britain was already richer than many other nations, with fertile well-farmed land, a flourishing cloth industry and expanding trade. Between **c.1750-1850**, this wealth increased, as new industries developed, transformed by the invention of machines powered by steam and water. This is known as the Industrial Revolution. Improved agriculture played a part, and advances in banking, foreign trade and transportation by road, rail and canal made the movement of goods cheaper and more efficient. In the 19th century other European countries, especially Germany, began industrializing too, followed by the United States and Japan.

Spinning Jenny

1767 James Hargreaves, British inventor, invents the "Spinning Jenny", which can spin up to 8 threads at a time.

1768 France buys Corsica from Genoa.

1769 Richard Arkwright, British cotton manufacturer, invents the water frame, a water-powered spinning machine.

Arkwright's water frame

1772 Slavery is declared illegal in Britain.

1773 Pope Clement XIV suppresses the Jesuit order.

1774 Joseph Priestley, a British scientist, isolates oxygen, which he calls "dephlogisticated air".

1776 Adam Smith (1723-1790), Scottish economist, publishes *The Wealth of Nations*, advocating free trade and private enterprise.

1777 James Watt, Scottish engineer, designs a steam engine, which leads to use of steam power in industry.

James Watt's steam engine

1778 France and Holland declare war on Britain in support of American colonists.

1779 Antoine Lavoisier, French scientist, names oxygen.

1779 France and Spain unsuccessfully besiege Gibraltar.

Northern and Eastern Europe

1762-1796 Reign of Catherine II ("the Great") of Russia. A German princess, she marries the heir to the throne, Peter III, and is a party to his murder. Under her rule, Russia extends its boundaries, Russian culture develops and St. Petersburg becomes a magnificent city. She introduces reforms in government and allows religious freedom.

Catherine the Great's crown and brooch

1768-1774 War between Russia and Turkey.

1769 Austria seizes the Polish territories of Lvov and Zips.

c.1770s Great age of European orchestral music begins: Haydn (1732-1809), Mozart (1756-1791) and Beethoven (1770-1827).

Salzburg cathedral

Mozart at the piano with his father

1771-1792 Reign of Gustavus III of Sweden.

1772 First partition of Poland by Russia, Prussia and Austria. Russia makes modest gains. Prussia annexes most of the territory between Pomerania and Eastern Prussia. Austria annexes a large area north of Hungary.

1772 Gustavus III of Sweden forces through a new constitution giving himself greater power.

Marquee built for Gustavus III

1773-1775 Peasant uprisings in Russia, led by Cossack Pugachev.

1774 Treaty of Kuchuk-Kainarji ends Russo-Turkish war. Russia gains Black Sea ports and the right to represent Christians in the Ottoman empire.

Africa to India

1761 Battle of Panipat: the Afghans defeat the Marathas.

1761-1790 Rise of Sikhs in India.

THE BRITISH IN INDIA

The British victory at Plassey in 1757 gave the East India Company effective control of Bengal, the richest area of India, and of Calcutta, its major port. In 1761, they captured Pondicherry from the French, marking the final collapse of French power in India. The Company's prosperity grew steadily. Land and privileges were obtained from wealthy native rulers, in return for support and protection. A series of wars brought more territory, as well as recognition of British sovereignty. In 1764, Clive was appointed governor and commander-in-chief in Bengal, and in 1773 Warren Hastings became first governor-general of British India. India became so important to Britain that, in 1784, the government took direct control of the political administration: a significant step towards colonization.

East India Company official with servants

1769-1772 James Bruce, Scottish explorer, visits Ethiopia.

1775-1782 British and Marathas at war.

c.1775 East Africa: Masai expand as far as Ngong Hills.

Masai cattle herders

The Far East

1767 Burmese invade Siam, destroy the capital, Ayutthaya, and take control of most of the country.

1767-1769 China invades Burma and war breaks out between them. Burma becomes a Chinese dependency.

1768 Taksin, a Siamese general, forms an army and drives out the Burmese. He defeats various local rulers and becomes the new King of Siam. His capital is at Thonburi.

COOK'S TRAVELS

James Cook, a British navigator, reached the Pacific island of Tonga and New Zealand in 1769, and the east coast of Australia (which he claimed for Britain) in 1770. He named the spot where he landed Botany Bay, because of the abundant plant life. Further trips (1772-1774 and 1776-1779) took him to New Hebrides and Hawaii.

Butterfly fish

Breadfruit

Captain Cook on his ship, the Endeavour

America and the Pacific

1760 Britain takes Montreal and controls St. Lawrence river.

A wrecked fur trade boat

1762 Britain captures Grenada and St. Vincent.

1763 Peace of Paris establishes British supremacy over French in North America.

1763 Rio de Janeiro becomes capital of Brazil.

1763 Proclamation Line in North America defines limits of settler expansion. All land west of it is reserved for Native North Americans.

1766 Britain occupies Falkland Islands.

1767 New British taxes on goods to North America upset the colonists.

1776 Spaniards found San Francisco.

THE AMERICAN WAR OF INDEPENDENCE

The American War of Independence (1775-1783) followed a decade of increasing dissatisfaction in the colonies with British rule. In 1770, violent anti-tax protests took place (the "Boston Massacre") and, in 1773, Bostonians threw chests of tea into the sea (the "Boston Tea Party"). In May 1775, representatives from the colonies met at the Philadelphia Congress, and in June 1776, an army was set up under George Washington. On July 4, 1776, Congress signed the Declaration of Independence and war broke out.

Paul Revere riding to warn fellow Americans that British troops are coming

1778 France and Spain ally with Americans against Britain.

1779 James Cook is killed in Hawaii.

1750

1779

Southern and Western Europe

1781 Joseph II of Austria (1780-1790) introduces religious toleration and major reforms, including abolition of serfs.

1784 William Pitt the Younger becomes Prime Minister.

1785 Edmund Cartwright, British clergyman, invents the power loom, which mechanizes weaving.

THE FRENCH REVOLUTION

In **May 1789**, facing mounting debts and growing unrest, Louis XVI called the national parliament for the first time since 1614. Parliament consisted of three Estates: Nobility, Clergy and Commoners, but on **June 17**, the Commoners formed their own National Assembly. This marked the start of the French Revolution. Fears that the King might dissolve the Assembly led to riots, and on **July 14**, the mob stormed and destroyed the infamous Bastille Prison. Revolution spread through France and many nobles fled abroad for safety. In **1792**, the National Convention replaced the National Assembly, and monarchy was abolished. In 1793, Louis XVI was executed and power passed to an extremist political group, the Jacobins, led by Maximilien Robespierre. The period 1793-1794 is known as the Reign of Terror: all those suspected of betraying the revolution were executed by guillotine. In **July 1794**, Robespierre himself was executed and France came under the control of a group called the Directory (1795-1799).

The storming of the Bastille on July 14th, 1789

1791 English politician William Wilberforce's bill for abolition of slavery is passed.

1791-1792 Thomas Paine writes *The Rights of Man*, supporting the ideas behind the French Revolution.

1793 France declares war on Britain, Netherlands and Spain.

1795 European coalition forms against France.

1796 Edward Jenner, British doctor, introduces vaccination against smallpox.

1796-1797 French troops conquer much of Italy. Republics are established in Rome and Switzerland in 1798.

1798 Unsuccessful rebellion against the British in Ireland, led by Irish Protestant Wolfe Tone.

1799 Napoleon Bonaparte takes control in France.

Northern and Eastern Europe

1781 Austro-Russian alliance against Turkey.

1783 Russia annexes the Crimea.

1784 Power struggle in Holland between the stadtholder, the Estates-General, and the Patriot party.

1787-1791 Russia goes to war with Turkey and gains the Black Sea Steppes.

1788 Austria declares war on Turkey and overruns Moldavia.

1788 Gustavus III of Sweden declares war on Russia.

Swedish soldier

1789 Revolt in Austrian Netherlands (Belgium) against centralizing policy of Joseph II. Proclamation of a Belgian Republic (1790), which is later reconquered by Austria.

1790-1792 Reign of Habsburg Emperor Leopold II.

Leopold II of Austria

1791 King of Poland adopts a new constitution to protect the country from Russian interference. Catherine II invades at the request of the nobles, destroys the constitution and divides large areas of Poland between Russia and Prussia.

1792 Gustavus III of Sweden is assassinated at a masked ball.

1792 France declares war on Austria and Prussia.

1793 Second partition of Poland. Russia takes the eastern territory inhabited by Ukrainians and White Russians. Prussia gains Danzig, Thorn and Posen and expands its eastern frontier.

1794 Polish uprising suppressed by Russia.

1794 France occupies the Netherlands, and renames it the Batavian Republic (1795-1806).

1795 Poland disappears after the third partition. Prussia takes Warsaw, Austria takes West Galicia, and Russia gains the remaining territory, including Lithuania.

| | Poland | Russian gains | Prussian gains | Austrian gains |

The 2nd partition of Poland in 1793

The 3rd partition of Poland in 1795

Africa to India

1784 India Act: British government takes control of political affairs in British India.

1786 Ottoman Turks send a fleet to restore control in Egypt, after period of unrest.

1787 British establish a colony for freed slaves in Sierra Leone.

c.1790 East Africa: Buganda kingdom expands its frontiers.

1794 Aga Muhammed founds the Qaja dynasty in Persia, which lasts until 1925.

1795-1797 West Africa: Mungo Park, a British explorer, reaches Segu and Niger river.

Mungo Park

The sextant, which enabled early explorers to navigate accurately

1795-1796 British take Cape of Good Hope, South Africa, and Ceylon (Sri Lanka) from the Dutch.

1798-1799 Napoleon invades Egypt. Defeated by British at Battle of the Nile (1798), but defeats Turks at Aboukir Bay (1799).

Napoleon Bonaparte

1799 Rosetta Stone is found in Egypt: the key to understanding Egyptian hieroglyphs.

1799 British control South India. Tippoo, ruler of Mysore (1750-1799), is killed fighting the British.

Tippoo's tiger, a musical toy showing a tiger attacking a European, from Seringapatam, capital of Mysore

The Far East

1782 Siam: Taksin is deposed and executed after a rebellion. Prince Chakri seizes the throne and becomes Rama I, first king of the Chakri dynasty. He moves the capital to Bangkok. Siam grows in prosperity, the only Southeast Asian country to remain uncolonized by Europeans in the 19th century.

1783-1823 Burmese capital moves to Amarapura.

1785 François de la Pérouse, French explorer, leaves for the Pacific, in search of the Solomon Islands.

1786 English East India Company sets up base in Penang, Malaysia: first British settlement in Southeast Asia.

1787 Severe famine and rice riots in Edo (Tokyo), Japan.

The city of Edo, Japan, in the 18th century

1788 François de la Pérouse lands on the coast of New South Wales, Australia, a day after the British had established a colony there.

1788/1778 Convicts are transported from Britain to Sydney, the first British settlement in Australia.

1791-1792 China and Tibet at war.

1795 Matthew Flinders and George Bass, British explorers, make first trip inland from east coast of Australia.

America and the Pacific

1780 British capture Charleston, South Carolina.

1780-1783 Tupac Amaru, the last of the Incas, leads the Peruvian Indians in an unsuccessful revolt against the Spaniards.

1781 British General Cornwallis surrenders at Yorktown.

1783 Treaty of Paris: Britain recognizes independence of the 13 Colonies, renamed United States of America. Britain gives Florida to Spain.

Map of the United States in 1783

1787 New constitution is drawn up in United States by Thomas Jefferson.

1789-1797 George Washington is first President of the United States.

A bald eagle, used on the seal of the United States

1791 Canada Act: Canada is divided into English and French-speaking territories.

1791 Slave revolt in Haiti against the French, led by Toussaint L'Ouverture. He is Lieutenant Governor in 1796.

Toussaint L'Ouverture

1797 Britain takes Trinidad from Spain.

1798 Spaniards found Los Angeles, California.

Troupe de

THE
19th CENTURY

1800-1899

Europe

1800 Alessandro Volta, Italian physicist, invents the battery.

1801 Act of Union unites Britain and Ireland.

1804 Richard Trevithick, British engineer, builds first steam train to run on a track.

THE RISE OF NAPOLEON

A young Corsican general named Napoleon Bonaparte rose to power in France after winning a dazzling reputation on campaigns in Italy and Egypt. In 1799, he appointed himself First Consul (effectively military dictator) and disbanded the corrupt and ineffective Directory, and in 1804, crowned himself Emperor. Napoleon was a succesful statesman and administrator, introducing the *Code Napoléon* in 1804, confirming property rights granted to peasants by the Revolution. In 1805, Britain, Austria, Russia and Sweden allied against him, but he won important victories at Austerlitz (1805), Jena (1806) and Friedland (1807). In 1806, he dissolved the Holy Roman Empire and reorganized the German states. He installed members of his family as rulers in Spain, Italy and Westphalia and in 1810 had his general, Jean Bernadotte, made heir to the Swedish throne. By 1812, most of Western Europe was under his control. But his enemies continued to oppose his ambitions, and finally brought about his fall.

1805 Battle of Trafalgar: the British, led by Admiral Nelson, defeat the French.

1808-1814 Peninsular War: Britain successfully supports resistance movement against the French in Spain.

1809 Russia gains Finland from Sweden.

1809 Jean de Lamarck, a French zoologist, publishes his theories on the changes in living things, based on a study of fossils.

1811 England: Luddites start smashing machines in protest at the Industrial Revolution.

1812 Napoleon invades Russia, but is forced back.

Napoleon's army was ill-prepared for the harsh Russian winter. Of 600,000 men, only about 30,000 returned.

1813 Austria, Prussia and Russia defeat Napoleon in Germany, causing the collapse of his rule in Germany, Italy and Holland.

1814 The Allies reach Paris: Napoleon is forced to abdicate and is imprisoned on the island of Elba. Louis XVIII is restored.

1815 The Hundred Days: Napoleon escapes from Elba and retakes power, but is defeated at Waterloo and imprisoned on the island of St. Helena in the middle of the Atlantic, where he dies.

1815 Congress of Vienna meets to settle post-war boundaries.

Africa and the Middle East

1801 Russia takes Georgia.

1802 Trutor and Somerville, British explorers, explore Bechuanaland (now Botswana).

1805 Mungo Park, a Scottish doctor, sets out to explore the River Niger.

1805-1848 Mehemet Ali massacres the ruling Mamelukes in Egypt and is installed as *pasha* (viceroy). His dynasty rules until 1952.

Mehemet Ali, at his palace in Alexandria. During his reign, Egypt was opened to European influences.

1806 Cape of Good Hope, South Africa, becomes a British colony (officially recognized in 1814).

1807 British politician William Wilberforce passes a law banning British ships from taking part in slavery.

1807 Sierra Leone and Gambia become British Crown Colonies.

1808 Import of African slaves into the U.S.A. is prohibited.

1810 West Africa: Yoruba kingdom breaks up.

1811 War between Russia and Persia.

Fath Ali, ruler of Persia, attacking a Russian soldier

1818 The Mfecane, or time of troubles, in southern Africa. Shaka the Great (c.1787-1828) organizes an army of 40,000 men into uniformed regiments called *impi*. He founds the Zulu empire which extends over much of southern Africa and many local tribes are driven north.

Zulu warriors

Asia

1800 British traders begin importing opium from India into China.

Opium poppies

1801 English East India Company takes Tanjore and the Carnatic coast, India.

1802 Siam (now Thailand) annexes Battambang, Cambodia.

1802 Wars in the Deccan lead to the supremacy of the English East India Company in India.

1802 Ceylon (now Sri Lanka) becomes a British Crown Colony.

1803 Mogul emperor accepts British protection.

1809-1824 Reign of King Rama II of Siam. Start of contact with Europe after a period of isolation.

1810 Britain takes Mauritius from France.

1811-1813 British occupy Dutch Java.

1817-1823 Anglo-Maratha Wars end in British victory, removing final barrier to British supremacy in India.

1817 Expansion of Burmese in Assam.

1818 Java is restored to the Dutch.

THE FOUNDING OF SINGAPORE

Singapore was founded in 1819 by Sir Stamford Raffles, as a base for the English East India Company. Strategically situated, at the opening of the Malacca Straits, it was chosen to rival the Dutch port of Malacca in Malaya. Raffles negotiated with the island's ruler and established a colony. Despite being disease-ridden and virtually uninhabited, Singapore grew to become the largest and most prosperous port in the region, and played an important part in the expansion of British influence in Asia.

Map of the East Indies

British | Dutch

Penang
Kuala Lumpur
Malacca
Singapore
South China Sea
PHILIPPINES
BORNEO
SUMATRA
JAVA
INDONESIA

America and Australasia

1802-1803 The Australian coast is surveyed by English navigator, Matthew Flinders.

A grey kangaroo, one of the unusual animals Europeans found in Australia

1803 Lousiana Purchase: U.S. buys French land in North America.

1803 Britain acquires British Guiana, Tobago and St. Lucia.

1804 Hobart, Tasmania, is founded.

1808 Uprisings against the Spaniards begin in New Spain.

1808-1825 Wars of independence from Spanish and Portuguese colonial rule in South and Central America. Argentina (Provinces of Rio de la Plata) declares independence in 1810, Paraguay and Venezuela in 1811, Colombia in 1813, Uruguay in 1814 and Chile in 1816.

VENEZUELA
BRITISH GUIANA
NEW GRANADA
COLOMBIA
ECUADOR
DUTCH GUIANA
FRENCH GUIANA
PERU
BRAZIL
PACIFIC OCEAN
BOLIVIA
PARAGUAY
CHILE
URUGUAY
ARGENTINA
FALKLAND ISLANDS

Great Colombia 1819-1830

Provinces of Rio de la Plata

South America in the 19th century

1812-1814 Trade war between the U.S.A. and Britain.

1816 Argentina wins formal independence from Spain.

1816-1824 Simón Bolívar, Venezuelan rebel leader, and José de San Martín, another rebel leader, help to win independence for many colonies.

1818 A boundary is established between the U.S.A. and Canada.

1818 Chile becomes independent.

1819-1830 The state of Great Colombia is set up under Bolívar. It becomes independent from Spain in 1822.

1819 Spain loses Florida to the United States.

Europe

1820 Hans Oersted, a Danish scientist, shows that an electric current has a magnetic effect on a compass needle.

1820 Revolutions in Spain and Portugal.

1821 Napoleon dies on the island of St. Helena.

THE GREEK WAR OF INDEPENDENCE

During the 19th century, many countries struggled for independence from foreign rule, asserting their national identity. The first successful nationalist struggle was the Greek War of Independence (1821-1829). Supported by Britain, Russia and Austria, the Greeks won independence from the Ottoman empire at the Treaty of Adrianople (1829) and in 1832 Prince Otto of Bavaria became their first king.

1825 First passenger railway, from Stockton to Darlington, England.

1826 J-N Niepce (France) takes the world's first photograph.

1827 Battle of Navarino: Greece's allies destroy the Turkish fleet.

1829 George and Robert Stephenson, British engineers, build the *Rocket*, a steam engine, which reaches a top speed of 30 miles per hour.

Stephenson's Rocket pulling passenger cars

1829 English Metropolitan Police founded by Sir Robert Peel.

1830 Belgium wins independence.

1830 July Revolution in France installs Louis Philippe as king.

1831 Michael Faraday, English scientist, produces electric current from a moving magnet, using a disc dynamo.

1832 Reform Act in Britain gives the middle classes the vote.

1834-1839 Carlist Wars in Spain: Don Carlos, the pretender, attempts to gain the throne.

1834-1871 Charles Babbage designs an analytical engine, the first computer, helped by program designer Ada Lovelace.

1836 Britain: Chartists demand the vote for all adult males.

1837-1901 Reign of Queen Victoria of Great Britain.

1837 First electric telegraph invented by W. Cooke and C. Wheatstone (British).

1838 First practical photographic process produced by Louis Daguerre (French). His pictures are called daguerreotypes.

Africa and the Middle East

1820-1821 Egypt conquers the Sudan.

1822 U.S.A. founds Liberia, West Africa, as a colony for freed African slaves.

1823 William Wilberforce helps found the Anti-Slavery Society, which campaigns to abolish slavery. Slavery is abolished in the British empire in 1833.

1823-1831 War between the British and the Ashanti in Ghana.

1824 René Caillié, French explorer, sets out for Timbuktu in West Africa.

René Caillié (right) walking through the African jungle

1826-1828 War between Persia and Russia. Russia gains Armenian provinces.

1830 French forces conquer Algiers.

1831-1840 Syria and Lebanon are occupied by Egypt.

1835 Tripoli, Libya, becomes an Ottoman province.

1835-1837 Great Trek of Boers (Dutch settlers) from Cape of Good Hope, South Africa.

Zulu warriors attacking Dutch settlers, known as Boers, during the Great Trek

1838 Boers defeat Zulus at Battle of Blood River, Natal.

1838 War between the British and Afghans.

1839 Dutch settlers found the Republic of Natal.

1839 Britain takes Aden.

Asia

Map of Southeast Asia

1821 Siam invades the Malay state of Kedah.

1824-1826 First Anglo-Burmese War. British take Lower Burma and Assam.

1825-1830 Java War: Indonesians revolt against Dutch rule.

1830 English East India Company takes Mysore, India.

1833 English East India Company trade monopoly with India and China is abolished.

A clipper, a ship developed in the U.S.A. in the 1820s, for trade with the East

1839-1842 Opium War between Britain and China.

THE OPIUM WARS

In **1838**, Emperor Tao-kuang of China sent an official, Lin Tse-hsu, to Canton to prohibit the importation and use of Indian opium. Lin burned 20,000 chests of opium and drove British traders out of Canton to Hong Kong. This attempt to ban the trade in opium led to the outbreak of war in **1839**. The British fleet blockaded the Chinese coast and defeated Chinese resistance. By the Treaty of Nanking of **1842**, the Chinese were forced to open five ports to British trade. Britain also acquired Hong Kong.

Indians carrying an opium chest. British traders used opium to pay for Chinese goods.

America and Australasia

1821 Mexico is proclaimed independent. Agustin Iturbide becomes Emperor Agustin I in **1822**.

1822 Haiti is independent.

1822 Brazil declares independence and is ruled by King Pedro I.

1823 Monroe Doctrine in U.S.A.: President Monroe warns Europeans not to interfere in American affairs.

1823 Formation of the United Provinces of Central America (see map below).

1823-1824 Emperor Agustin I is overthrown and Mexico becomes a republic.

1825 Simón Bolívar founds Bolivia.

1826 The Black War in Tasmania between settlers and aborigines (the native people).

Aborigine

Rainbow Lorikeet, found in Australia

1828 Uruguay, part of Argentina since 1816, becomes a republic.

1829 Swan River Settlement founded in Western Australia.

c.**1830s** U.S. settlers move West, driving many Native North Americans from their homes.

Native North American teepee

1830 Colombia, Venezuela and Ecuador become independent republics.

1833 Britain takes Falkland Islands.

1834 Tolpuddle Martyrs, six English workers, are sent to Australia for trying to set up a Trade Union.

1834 British settlement at Port Philip Bay (Melbourne).

1835-1836 Rebels in Texas (part of Mexico) fight for independence. Texan rebels are massacred by Mexican forces at the Alamo mission station. Texas breaks away and forms a republic.

Map of United Provinces of Central America

1839-1840 El Salvador, Honduras, Nicaragua, Guatemala and Costa Rica become independent republics.

1820

1839

81

Europe

1840 First postage stamp, the Penny Black, issued in Britain.

1845-1848 Irish famine leads to mass emigration to U.S.A.

1847 Civil war in Switzerland.

1848: THE YEAR OF REVOLUTIONS

In 1848, a wave of revolutions swept through Europe - with uprisings in Sicily, Paris, Vienna, Berlin, Milan, Sardinia, Warsaw and Prague. In France and Austria there had been growing opposition to conservative rulers, as well as economic difficulties - food shortages and rising prices. In Italy, Hungary, Bohemia and Poland, nationalist feeling was stirred by resentment of Habsburg rule. In Germany and Italy, there were also calls to found new nations by joining together the separate states. Both the French and Habsburg emperors were forced to abdicate, but in the end the rebellions were unsuccessful and short-lived, except in France. After temporary panic, the old regimes managed to reassert themselves.

The retaking of the Pantheon, Paris, by government troops

1848-1851 Second Republic in France.

1848 *Communist Manifesto* issued by Karl Marx and Friedrich Engels.

Karl Marx

1849 Austria wins back her Italian possessions, after defeating Piedmont-Sardinia.

1849 Guiseppe Garibaldi, Italian nationalist leader, marches to Rome, but his revolt is crushed.

1851 Great Exhibition (international trade fair) in London.

1852-1870 Second Empire in France: reign of Napoleon III.

THE CRIMEAN WAR

In 1853, Russia demanded the right to use the Dardanelles Straits for her ships, and to protect Turkish Christians. Turkey, France and Britain felt this gave Russia too much power and in 1854, declared war. After much bloodshed on both sides, Russia was forced to make concessions at the Treaty of Paris in 1856.

The Charge of the Light Brigade at the Battle of Balaklava

1859 Charles Darwin, English naturalist, publishes his theory of evolution in *On the Origin of the Species by Natural Selection*.

1859 Piedmont-Sardinia leads Italian uprising against Austria.

Africa and the Middle East

1841 David Livingstone, a Scottish missionary, makes his first journey of exploration in Africa.

David Livingstone

1841 Egypt loses Syria to Turkey.

1842 Boers establish the Orange Free State, South Africa.

1842-1843 Wars between Boers and British in Natal. Natal becomes a British colony.

1844 War between France and Morocco.

1846-1847 British defeat Bantus (Africans) in South Africa.

Boers and cannon

1847 Liberia becomes independent.

1852-1856 David Livingstone becomes first European to walk all the way across Africa. In 1855, he discovers the Victoria Falls, southern Africa.

1853 Richard Burton, British explorer, reaches holy city of Mecca in Arabia, forbidden to non-Muslims.

Burton disguised as an Arab at a Bedouin camp

1854 Orange Free State is recognized as a Boer republic.

1856 Pretoria becomes the capital of Transvaal, South Africa.

1856 Richard Burton and John Speke leave England in search of the source of the Nile.

1858 John Speke reaches the source of the Nile: Lake Victoria in East Africa.

Speke on the shore of Lake Victoria

1858-1864 David Livingstone explores the Zambezi river.

1859-1869 Suez Canal is built in Egypt.

Asia

1842 British conquer Labuan, Borneo.

1843 British conquer Sind, India.

1845-1846 First Anglo-Sikh War: British gain control of the Punjab.

1847 French expedition to Cochin China.

1848-1849 Second Anglo-Sikh War: British add the Punjab to their territory in India.

Indian woman waving British flag

1850-1864 Taiping Rebellion in China against the decaying Manchu dynasty.

1852 Second Anglo Burmese War.

1853 United States gunboats force Japan to open its ports to foreign trade. European contacts increase. A time of growing unrest and weakness for the Tokugawa dynasty.

Europeans from a Japanese print

1856 English East India Company takes Oudh.

Sword with East India Company crest

1856-1860 Second Opium War between Britain and China.

1857-1860 Anglo-French forces occupy Beijing, China.

THE INDIAN MUTINY

In 1857-1858 there was a series of uprisings against the British, which became known as the Indian Mutiny. It began in Meerut as a protest by Bengali soldiers in the British army, but soon spread throughout northern India, lasting over a year. After the relief of Lucknow (where British residents had been trapped for months), the British reasserted control. The government took over from the East India Company and administered India directly, through a viceroy, and the Mogul emperor was forced to give up his throne. India became the keystone of the British empire, and a focus for imperial rivalry, especially after the Russians began expanding in Central Asia.

A battle during the Indian Mutiny

1858 Treaty of Tientsin: 11 Chinese ports are opened to European trade.

1859-1865 Mandalay becomes the capital of Burma.

America and Australasia

1840 Captain Wilkes, American explorer, discovers the Antarctic coast.

1840 Treaty of Waitangi: native Maori chiefs give up sovereignty over New Zealand to Britain.

Maori warrior and sword

1840 Upper and Lower Canada united. Given self-government under British monarch in 1841.

1843 New telegraph code is designed by Samuel Morse (U.S.A.), replacing the one used by Cooke and Wheatstone.

1844-1845 Charles Sturt, English explorer, leads an expedition into Central Australia.

1844-1848 Unsuccessful uprisings in New Zealand by Maoris against the British.

1845 Texas and Florida become states of the U.S.A.

1846-1848 War between Mexico and U.S.A over boundaries. Mexico loses California, New Mexico, Arizona, Utah and Colorado.

1848-1849 Gold is discovered in California. This leads to a huge rush to the west by settlers in search of gold.

1848 Otago, New Zealand, is founded.

1851 Gold is discovered at Bathurst, Victoria.

1851 Isaac Singer (U.S.A.) produces the first practical sewing machine.

American settlers heading west in the Gold Rush

1853-1854 Gold rush in Victoria, Australia.

1857 Civil war in Mexico.

1859 Queensland, Australia, becomes a separate colony.

1859 Oil is discovered in Pennsylvania, which leads to the start of the modern oil industry.

Europe

THE UNIFICATION OF ITALY

Until the 19th century, Italy was just a collection of states, some independent, some under foreign rule. Unification came about mainly because of the ambitions of one of the states, Piedmont-Sardinia, and its chief minister, Camillo Cavour. In 1859, Piedmont won Lombardy from Austria, and in 1860 most of northern Italy voted to join them. Giuseppe Garibaldi led a revolt against the Spanish Bourbon rulers in southern Italy, and joined it to the Italian kingdom. In 1861, Victor Emmanuel II of Piedmont-Sardinia became first king of Italy. Venice joined in 1866 and Rome in 1870.

Lombardy 1859
Venice 1866
Piedmont
Parma 1860
Romagna 1860
Modena 1860
Lucca 1860
Tuscany 1860
Naples 1860
Papal States 1860-1870
Sardinia
Sicily 1860

1861 Alexander II of Russia frees the serfs (landless peasants).

1863 World's first underground railway is built in London.

1864 Red Cross Society founded in Geneva, to care for war casualties.

1865 Louis Pasteur, French doctor, publishes his germ theory.

1866 War between Austria and Italy. Italy gains Venice.

1866 Gregor Mendel, Bohemian botanist, publishes his laws of inheritance.

Mendel performed experiments on sweet pea plants.

1867 The Austrian empire is renamed the Austro-Hungarian empire.

1867 Prussia, led by minister Otto von Bismarck, forms the Confederation of North German states.

1867 Joseph Lister, British surgeon, describes use of antiseptics to reduce infections.

1867 Second Reform Act extends the right to vote in Britain.

1867 Karl Marx publishes *Das Kapital*, outlining his theories.

1870 Irish Land Act gives Irish tenants compensation for eviction.

1870-1871 Franco-Prussian War. Prussians overthrow Second Empire. Revolution sets up the Third Republic (1870-1940).

1871 Paris Commune (a revolutionary group) is crushed.

1871 Germany is united. Wilhelm I of Prussia becomes first Kaiser (emperor), with Bismarck as Chancellor.

1872-1874 Civil war in Spain.

1873 Home Rule League founded to promote Irish self-rule.

1873 Alliance of Russia, Germany and Austria-Hungary.

1874 Iceland becomes independent.

1877-1878 Russo-Turkish War ends in Congress of Berlin. Romania, Montenegro and Serbia win independence.

1878 Joseph Swan, British scientist, invents a light bulb.

1879 Dual Alliance between Germany and Austria-Hungary.

Africa and the Middle East

1860 French begin expanding settlements in West Africa.

1869 Diamond rush begins in South Africa.

1869 Tunisia is controlled by Britain, France and Italy.

1869 Suez Canal in Egypt is opened.

1871 Ujiji, East Africa: Sir Henry Stanley, journalist, meets David Livingstone, an explorer who has been missing four years.

Stanley meeting Livingstone

1872 British take over Dutch forts on Gold Coast (Ghana).

1873-1874 British and Ashanti at war in Gold Coast.

1874-1877 Sir Henry Stanley explores the Congo.

1875 British Prime Minister Disraeli buys majority shares in the Suez Canal, ensuring control of the sea route to India.

1876 Britain and France take control of Egypt's finances.

1877 Britain annexes the Transvaal.

1879 Britain and France control Egypt.

1879 Zulus defeat British at Battle of Isandlhwana, Natal, but are defeated at Ulundi.

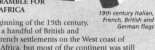

19th century Italian, French, British and German flags

THE SCRAMBLE FOR AFRICA

At the beginning of the 19th century, there was a handful of British and French settlements on the West coast of Africa, but most of the continent was still unknown to Europeans. The only established colonies were Angola and Mozambique (Portuguese), Cape Colony (which passed from Dutch to British control in 1814) and Algeria (French). However, between 1877 and 1914 most of Africa was colonized by European powers. It happened so fast it became known as the "Scramble for Africa". There were many reasons for the scramble. Industrialization and expanding world trade produced a demand for new markets and materials. Exploration and the railways opened up new areas for development. Some colonies were acquired almost by accident, as a result of land-grabbing by men on the spot, such as Cecil Rhodes, founder of De Beers, the diamond mining company. But European rivalries also played a big part. Africa was the last continent to be opened up, and new nations, such as Germany, Italy and Belgium, saw it as an opportunity to acquire an empire.

Guineas, named after Guinea, in West Africa, where the gold was mined

Cecil Rhodes

Asia

1860 British and French forces burn down the Summer Palace, Beijing. Second Opium War between Britain and China comes to an end. China cedes Kowloon to Britain.

1861-1862 France goes to war with Cochin-China (South Vietnam) and establishes a protectorate over the province by 1867.

1862-1908 Dowager Empress Tz'u-hsi rules China, on behalf of her baby son.

Summer Palace, Beijing, rebuilt by Empress Tz'u-hsi

1863 France establishes a protectorate in Cambodia.

1865 Russia expands in Central Asia, taking the khanate of Tashkent.

1868 Russia takes the khanate of Bukhara, Central Asia.

1868 The major clans in Japan organize opposition to the Tokugawas. The last shogun, Kei-ki, abdicates after a coup d'état and the emperor's power is restored under a new government (the Meiji Restoration 1868-1912). A period of growth and modernization.

The young Emperor returning to Edo, to take power from the shogun

1873 Russia acquires Khiva and provinces of Central Asia.

Map of the expansion of Russia into Central Asia in the 19th century

Russian empire 1815
Added by 1856
Added by 1876
Added by 1900

RUSSIA

KAZAKHSTAN

Khiva • • Tashkent

TURKMENISTAN • Samarkand
Bukhara

CHINA

PERSIA

AFGHANISTAN INDIA

Subject states

1874 Annam (now part of Vietnam) is opened to French trade. Tonkin is made a French protectorate in 1883.

1876 Korea is declared independent by China.

1877 Queen Victoria of Great Britain is proclaimed Empress of India.

1878-1880 War between Britain and Afghanistan. British India makes frontier gains and British influence in Afghanistan grows.

America and Australasia

1860s-1870s Wars with settlers lead to huge reduction in population of Native North Americans.

An Apache spear

1860-1861 Robert Burke and William Wills, British explorers, cross Australia.

1860-1864 War between Maoris (native peoples) and settlers in New Zealand.

THE AMERICAN CIVIL WAR

In 1860, Abraham Lincoln, a firm supporter of the abolition of slavery, was elected U.S. President. The following year, in 1861, the southern states, whose economy was dependent on slavery, broke away and formed the Confederate States of America. A bloody civil war broke out with the northern Unionists, who fought to preserve national unity. After bitter fighting, with 635,000 people killed, the Unionists finally defeated the Confederates in 1865.

Abraham Lincoln

1863 Battle of Gettysburg. Unionist victory - Confederate General "Stonewall" Jackson, is killed.

1863 Gold rush in New Zealand.

1864 France installs Archduke Maximilian of Austria as Emperor of Mexico. He is shot in 1867.

1865 Slavery abolished in the U.S.A. Lincoln is assassinated.

1866 First transatlantic cable.

1867 United States buys Alaska from Russia for $7 million.

1867 Canada becomes a dominion (a self-governing colony).

1868 14th Amendment gives civil rights to African-Americans in the U.S.A.

1868-1878 Cuba loses war of independence against Spain.

1869 First U.S. trans-continental railroad built.

1876 Battle of Little Big Horn (or "Custer's Last Stand"): Native American Sioux and Cheyenne warriors defeat U.S. army, led by Colonel George Custer.

1876 Telephone is patented in the U.S.A. by Alexander G. Bell.

A Bell telephone in use

1877 Thomas Edison, a U.S. inventor, invents the record player.

1877-1911 Rule of Porfirio Diaz, Mexican dictator. He establishes order, wealth and prosperity.

1879 Thomas Edison invents a light bulb.

1879-1884 Chile expands territory after war with Bolivia and Peru.

1860

1879

Europe

86

1880-1885 Unrest in Ireland.

1881 Russia: Alexander II is assassinated. Repression follows.

1883 Russian Marxist Party is founded. Unrest follows.

1884 Reform Act in Britain gives the vote to all men over 21.

1885 Karl Benz, German engineer, builds the first motor car.

First Benz car

Fuel tank

Engine

1886 Gladstone's First Home Rule Bill for Ireland is defeated.

1888-1918 Reign of Kaiser Wilhelm II of Germany.

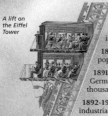

A lift on the Eiffel Tower

1889 Eiffel Tower is built for the Paris Exposition.

1890 Luxembourg becomes independent from Holland.

1890s Art Nouveau style is popular in Europe.

1891-1896 Otto Lilienthal, German engineer, makes over a thousand flights in his gliders.

1892-1903 Modernization and industrial growth in Russia under Sergei Witte (finance minister).

1893 Britain: Keir Hardie founds Independent Labour Party.

1893 France allies with Russia.

1894 Nicholas II becomes Tsar of Russia.

1894 Dreyfus Affair in France. Alfred Dreyfus, a Jewish army officer, is expelled for treason. Many believe he is innocent and it leads to a political battle. (He is cleared in 1906.)

1894-1897 Cretans rise against Turks and unite with Greece.

1895 Guglielmo Marconi, Italian physicist, invents wireless.

1895 Sigmund Freud, Austrian psychiatrist, publishes his first work on psychoanalysis.

1895 Wilhelm Röntgen, German physicist, discovers x-rays.

1896 First modern Olympic Games in Athens, Greece.

1895 Motion pictures are premiered in Paris, France.

1898 Pierre and Marie Curie, French scientists, observe radioactivity and isolate radium.

Caricature of Pierre and Marie Curie

Africa and the Middle East

1880-1881 First Anglo-Boer War: Boer victory at Majuba Hill. Britain forced to recognize independent Transvaal.

1880-1900 French influence grows in the Sahara region.

French Saharan soldier

1881-1882 Nationalist revolt in Egypt. British forces occupy Egypt and Sudan, to suppress anti-European riots.

1881 Tunisia becomes a French colony.

1884 Anti-British uprising in the Sudan, led by the Mahdi, a religious leader. General Gordon is sent to Khartoum.

Map of the Sudan

EGYPT

AFRICA

SUDAN

Khartoum ●

Fashoda ●

Area under Mahdi's control 1881-1898

General Gordon

1884 Britain takes British Somaliland. Germany takes South West Africa, Cameroons and Togo.

1885 The Mahdi takes Khartoum and Gordon is killed.

1885 Britain takes Bechuanaland (Botswana). Germany takes Tanganyika. Italy takes Eritrea. Belgium takes Belgian Congo. Spain takes Rio de Oro and Spanish Guinea.

1886 Royal Niger Company given control of British territories in Nigeria. Lagos and Kenya become British colonies.

1886 Gold found in Transvaal. Johannesburg is founded.

1888-1889 Cecil Rhodes's British South Africa Company expands British influence in Rhodesia (Zimbabwe).

1889 French take Ivory Coast. Italy takes Italian Somaliland and claims a protectorate over Ethiopia.

1890-1897 Armenian anti-Turkish revolutionary movement.

1891 Emperor Menelik of Ethiopia rejects Italian protectorate. Italians invade in 1895, but are forced to recognize Ethiopian independence.

1894 French take Dahomey.

1895 British take Uganda.

1895-1896 Jameson Raid in South Africa: a failed attempt by Cecil Rhodes to take over the Transvaal.

1896 French annex Madagascar.

1898 Fashoda Crisis: French advancing north meet British advancing south at Fashoda, Sudan. French withdraw. Battle of Omdurman: British defeat Sudanese.

1899 British government takes control of Nigerian territories. Sudan comes under Anglo-Egyptian rule.

1899-1902 Second Anglo-Boer War. Britain annexes the Transvaal and Orange Free State.

Queen Victoria's South Africa medal, awarded to British soldiers who fought in the Boer War

Asia

1883 Annam, in Indochina, becomes a French protectorate.

1883-1884 The French expand in Southeast Asia.

1884 Russia takes Turkmenistan.

1884 Cambodia is annexed by France.

1885 The founding of the Indian National Congress, which campaigns for independence.

A spinning wheel, the symbol of the Indian National Congress

1885 1886 The British attack and annex Ava in Burma.

Indian army troops fighting in Upper Burma

1887 France establishes an Indo-Chinese Union.

1894-1895 War between Japan and China. Japan gains Formosa. Korea becomes independent of China.

1896 Britain sets up the Federated Malay States.

1896 Rebellion against the Spanish in the Philippines.

1897 Anglo-Siamese agreement on Malaya-Siam boundary.

19th century Siamese king

1898 War between Spain and the U.S.A. over the Philippines. Spain cedes Philippines to the U.S.A.

1898-1909 Reactionary and repressive rule in China under Empress Tz'u-hsi. Attempts at liberal reforms are crushed.

America and Australasia

1880 Start of the construction of the Panama Canal.

1886 Statue of Liberty is completed in New York.

The Statue of Liberty (below)

1887 Emile Berliner (1851-1929), a German who emigrated to the U.S.A., patents the gramophone.

Berliner's gramophone

1888 George Eastman (U.S.A.) mass markets his box camera, making photography more accessible.

1889 Pedro II of Brazil is deposed and a republic set up.

1890 Battle of Wounded Knee: last Native American uprising in the U.S.A. by the Sioux people. The Native Americans are defeated and their weapons taken away.

Many tribes were rounded up and taken to live on special areas of land called reservations.

Many Sioux warriors wore special "ghost shirts", believing they could protect them from the settlers' bullets

1893 Hawaii becomes a U.S. protectorate.

1893 Women in New Zealand become the first in the world to be given the vote

1898 Spanish-American War. Cuba becomes independent under temporary American control.

THE
20th CENTURY

1900-1999

Europe

1901 Great Britain: death of Queen Victoria and accession of Edward VII.

Queen Victoria

1902 Britain allies with Japan: the end of a long period of Japanese isolation.

1903 King and Queen of Serbia are assassinated.

1903 French minister Delcassé visits London. Growing Anglo-French friendship.

1904 *Entente Cordiale*: friendship pact between Britain and France.

1905 Revolts in St. Petersburg and other Russian cities. In St. Petersburg, soldiers open fire on protesters.

1905 Norway becomes independent from Sweden.

1905 Albert Einstein (Switzerland) publishes his Special Theory of Relativity.

Albert Einstein

1908 Austria-Hungary takes Turkish provinces Herzegovina and Bosnia. Tension follows. Bulgaria wins independence.

1908 Failed revolution in Portugal: the King and his heir are assassinated.

1910 Revolution in Portugal: the King is deposed. A republic is declared in 1911.

1911 Ernest Rutherford (N.Z./U.K.) shows that atoms have a nucleus.

Electron

Rutherford's model of an atom

Nucleus

1912 First Balkan War: Bulgaria, Greece, Serbia and Montenegro unite and defeat Turkey.

1913 Second Balkan War: Turkey, Romania, Serbia and Greece defeat Bulgaria.

Africa and the Middle East

Map showing European colonisation of African countries

Key:
- French
- British
- German
- Portugese
- Belgian
- Anglo Egyptian Condominium
- Spanish
- Italian

1900 South Africa: British annex Transvaal and Orange Free State. Anglo-Boer War ends with Peace of Vereeniging (1902).

1901 Britain joins Ashanti kingdom to the Gold Coast colony.

1909 Ahmed Shah seizes power in Persia, at the age of 11, after his elder brother Muhammed Ali is deposed.

1908 Belgium takes over Congo from Belgian King Leopold.

1908-1909 Revolution in Turkey by the Young Turks, a group of army officers, including Mustafa Kemâl. Sultan is deposed.

1910 Union of South Africa becomes a British dominion. French Congo is renamed French Equatorial Africa.

1911 Agadir crisis: Germans send a gunboat to Agadir, Morocco, provoking tensions with France.

1911-1912 Italians take Libya, after strugle with Turkey.

1914-1915 Germany loses colonies to Britain and France.

1914-1922 Egypt becomes a British protectorate.

THE FIRST WORLD WAR

At the start of the 20th century, the balance of power in Europe was so delicately balanced that an attack on one country would automatically involve its allies and lead to war. In **June 1914**, Archduke Franz Ferdinand, heir to the Austrian throne, was assassinated by a Serbian nationalist in Sarajevo. Austria declared war on Serbia, and within weeks, war had broken out between Germany and Austria (the Central Powers) and Russia, France and Britain (the Allies).

The First World War (1914-1918), or "Great War" as it was known at the time, was mainly a European war, fought across Europe and the

Middle East: much of the fighting took place in northern France, where each side dug trenches to stop the other from advancing. But many other nations, especially the colonies - and later the U.S.A. -became directly involved. It dragged on for four years, killing 17 million people - more than in any other conflict in history.

Dreadnought, the most powerful ship of its day

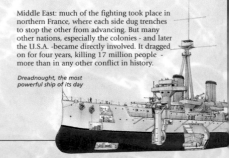

Poppies, a symbol of remembrance of the war

Asia

1900 Boxer Rebellion in China against foreign influence is crushed by an international force.

A dragon, ancient symbol of China

1904-1905 Russia and Japan at war over Manchuria and Korea.

1905 Japan destroys Russian fleet at Tsushima. Treaty of Portsmouth gives Japan a protectorate over Korea and territory in China.

Japanese painting showing the Russian defeat at Tsushima

1905 10,000 people die in earthquake in Lahore, India.

1909 Anglo-Siam Treaty: Siam recognizes British control over Malayan states.

1909 China occupies Tibet. The Tibetan ruler, the Dalai Lama, flees to India.

1910 Malayan states of Trengganu and Perlis accept British protection.

1910 China: uprising in Yunnan province.

1910 Nationalist movement in Burma led by Buddhist monks.

Tibetan monk playing a trumpet at a festival

1910-1945 Korea is a Japanese colony.

Japanese flag

1911 Chinese Revolution: a government is set up in Nanking under Sun Yat-sen.

1912 Chinese Manchu dynasty is overthrown and a republic is established. This is followed by a period of great unrest and local rule by warlords.

America and Australasia

1900 New Zealand takes the Cook Islands. Papua is transferred from Britain to Australia. Britain annexes Tonga.

1901 The Commonwealth of Australia is established.

1901 Guglielmo Marconi, Italian inventor, sends the first wireless transmission from U.S.A. to England.

1902 Australia: women win the right to vote.

1903 Revolution in Panama. Panama gains independence from Colombia as a U.S. protectorate.

1903 Orville and Wilbur Wright (U.S.A.) make the first successful powered and controlled flight.

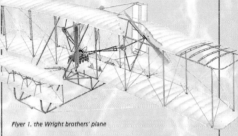

Flyer 1, the Wright brothers' plane

1906 San Francisco: earthquake followed by a fire destroys much of the city.

1907 New Zealand is given dominion (self-governing) status within the British empire.

1908-1918 Unrest in Haiti.

1909 Robert E. Peary and Matthew Henson of United States Navy claim to reach the North Pole.

Seals in the North Pole

1910-1911 Revolution in Mexico overthrows Porfirio Diaz. Followed by disorder and the rise of dictators.

1912 Sinking of ocean liner *Titanic* off the coast of Newfoundland

1912 Roald Amundsen, Norwegian explorer, is the first to reach the South Pole.

Penguins at the South Pole

Ford Model T, the first mass-produced car

1912-1913 Henry Ford (U.S.A.) begins the mass production of motor cars.

1914 The Panama canal is opened.

1915

Europe

1916 Easter Rising in Dublin: Irish nationalists against British.

THE RUSSIAN REVOLUTION

In **1900**, Russia was one of the most underdeveloped places in Europe. Most people lived in poverty, under the oppressive, autocratic rule of the tsars. World War One led to starvation and huge loss of life, which fed growing discontent. In **April 1917**, the leader of the communist Bolshevik party, Vladimir Ilyich Ulyanov (known as Lenin), returned to Russia from exile. His influence spread fast and in **October** he and his supporters stormed the palace in St Petersburg and seized power. The new government acted through a Congress of Soviets: they centralized control of the land, murdered the Tsar and his family, and held onto power through a campaign of fear, known as the "Red Terror". They won a civil war (**1918-1920**), despite support for their opponents, the Whites, from foreign powers anxious to stop the spread of revolution. In **1922**, Russia became the Union of Soviet Socialist Republics (U.S.S.R.).

Tsar Nicholas, Alexandra and children

1918 Peace of Brest-Litovsk between Russia and Germany.

1918-1919 Revolution in Berlin: the Kaiser flees. The German Weimar Republic is set up in 1919.

1918 Britain: the vote is given to women over 30.

1918-1919 Emperor of Austria-Hungary abdicates. New independent nations : Latvia, Estonia, Lithuania, Czechoslovakia and Yugoslavia.

1919 Peace of Versailles between Germany and the Allies.

1919 Benito Mussolini establishes Fascist movement in Italy.

1919 Ernest Rutherford (N.Z./U.K.) splits the atom.

1919 Solar eclipse (see below) confirms Einstein's theories.

1919 Finland becomes a republic.

1920 Six northern Irish counties set up parliament in Belfast. Irish Free State (the southern counties) becomes a British dominion from 1921.

1922 Benito Mussolini forms a Fascist government in Rome.

1923 De Rivera is Spanish dictator.

1926 Britain: 9-day General Strike.

1928 Alexander Fleming discovers penicillin, the first antibiotic.

1924-1953 Josef Stalin leads U.S.S.R.

1924 Greece becomes a republic.

1924 Ahmed Zogu seizes power in Albania.

1926-1935 Józef Piłsudski leads Poland.

1928 U.S.S.R.: Five Year Plan is launched: a period of rapid growth and industrialization.

1929

Africa and the Middle East

1916 Arab nationalists in the Hejaz, Saudi Arabia, rise against the Ottomans. Further uprisings follow.

1916 British Colonel T.E. Lawrence explores the Hejaz area of Saudi Arabia.

Colonel T.E. Lawrence

1917 Balfour Declaration: Britain supports Jewish homeland in Palestine, so long as Arab rights are respected.

Dome of the Rock, Jerusalem

1918 Syria proclaims independence. Not recognized by France or Britain. French forces take control in 1919.

1918 Ottoman empire collapses: Allies control Istanbul.

1919 War begins between Britain and Afghanistan.

1919 German African colonies are mandated to the Allies by the League of Nations.

1919 Egypt: nationalist revolt against British protectorate. Britain recognizes Egyptian independence in 1922.

1920 Transjordan is separated from Syria.

1920-1921 Uprising in Iraq. Britain installs an autonomous Arab government under King Faisal, brother of Abdullah, King of Jordan, and a member of the Hashemite dynasty.

1921 Moroccan Berbers defeat Spaniards at Anual.

1922 Mustafa Kemâl, or Atatürk, seizes power in Turkey. Greek army is expelled and Ottoman emperor deposed. Republic is proclaimed: reform and modernization follows.

Turkish flag and Mustafa Kemâl Atatürk

1922 France gains League of Nations mandate over Syria.

1923 Ethiopia joins the League of Nations.

1923 Southern Rhodesia (Zimbabwe) is formally annexed as a British colony.

1924-1925 Reza Khan becomes Shah of Persia.

1924 Moroccan independence movement grows, but is crushed by Spanish and French forces in 1926.

1926 Ibn Saud becomes King of Hejaz and Nejd (later Saudi Arabia).

1926 Lebanon becomes a republic.

1927 Britain recognizes Ibn Saud as the ruler of Saudi Arabia.

Benito Mussolini and the Fascist symbol: a bundle of twigs tied around an axe

Asia

1919 India: British soldiers under the command of General Dyer fire on protesters at a peaceful political meeting in Amritsar. Leads to a rise in Indian nationalist feeling. General Dyer is fired.

1920 Mohandas (Mahatma) Gandhi leads the Indian National Congress, a non-violent movement for independence. The first Indian Parliament meets in 1921.

Gandhi

1921 Mao Zedong (Mao Tse-tung) and Li Ta-chao form the Chinese Communist Party in Beijing.

Mao Zedong

1923 An earthquake and fire destroys much of Tokyo, Japan.

Tokyo after the earthquake

1925 China: Sun Yat-sen dies. He is succeeded by Jiang Jie Shi (Chiang Kai-shek), who campaigns against the warlords.

1926 Hirohito becomes Emperor of Japan.

1927 Jiang Jie Shi, leader of the Kuomintang (Chinese Nationalists), breaks with the Communist Party. Civil war follows. The Communists set up bases in remote areas.

1928 Jiang Jie Shi becomes President of China.

1929 Gandhi demands Indian independence and begins a campaign of civil disobedience.

America and Australasia

1917 A number of U.S. passenger ships are sunk by German U-boats (submarines). U.S.A. declares war on Germany, joined by some South American states and Cuba.

1918 World wide influenza epidemic kills 20 million. In the U.S.A. alone, 500,000 die.

1919 League of Nations is set up to preserve world peace.

1920 The U.S. Senate votes not to join the League of Nations. Prohibition of alcohol and women's suffrage are introduced in the U.S.A.

1923 Edwin Hubble (U.S.A.) proves the existence of other galaxies.

The Hubble telescope

1927 Canberra becomes the federal capital of Australia.

1927 *The Jazz Singer*, one of the first talking pictures, or movies, is made.

1927 Charles Lindbergh makes the first solo flight across the Atlantic.

1929 Hubble shows galaxies moving away from each other. Forms the basis of the Big Bang Theory.

1929 The Wall Street Crash: U.S. stock market collapses. The beginning of the Depression.

THE DEPRESSION

From 1929 until the mid 1930s, nearly every country in the world experienced an economic crisis, known as the Depression. There was falling production, declining incomes and mass unemployment. The U.S.A., Germany, Eastern Europe and many places in Africa, Asia and Latin America were worst affected.

Unemployed people lining up at a soup kitchen

The Chrysler building, New York, built between 1928 and 1930

LINE FOR
1¢ RESTAURANT
20 MEALS FOR 1¢
DONATIONS WANTED
HELP FEED THE HUNGRY
I WILL FEED 20
1¢ RESTAURANT
107 W 43RD ST

1915

1929

93

Europe

1930 U.S.S.R.: Stalin enforces collectivization of agriculture. Millions of kulaks, peasant farm owners who oppose this, are suppressed and murdered. Famine follows in 1932.

1931 Alphonso XIII leaves Spain and a republic is set up.

1931 Statute of Westminster defines rights of British dominions: major step in founding of the Commonwealth.

1932-1968 Antonio Salazar is Prime Minister and virtual dictator of Portugal.

1933 Germany: Berlin parliament, the Reichstag, burns down. Adolf Hitler, leader of the fascist Nazi Party, becomes Chancellor. He takes the title *Führer* (leader) in 1934.

1934-1939 Stalin crushes opposition in U.S.S.R.

1935 Germany increases its military strength.

1935 Nuremberg Laws: German Jews persecuted.

The Star of David, which German Jews were forced to wear (top), and a Nazi officer's badge

1936 Britain: Edward VIII abdicates to marry Mrs. Simpson, a divorcée.

1936 Germans occupy Rhineland.

1936 German-Italian Axis Pact.

1936-1939 The Spanish Civil War: General Franco, Nationalist leader, rebels against Republican government. Germany and Italy give him military aid. U.S.S.R. supports Republicans. Franco becomes dictator until his death in 1975.

1937 Southern Ireland becomes the sovereign state of Eire.

1938 Hitler occupies Austria and joins the two countries under the Anschluss. At the Munich Conference, Germany is granted Sudetenland (German-speaking Czech territory), on the condition that no further expansion is made.

1938 *Kristallnacht* ("the Night of Broken Glass"): Nazis attack thousands of Jewish shops and synagogues.

1939 Hahn and Strassman (German) discover nuclear fission.

1939 Mussolini seizes Albania.

Africa and the Middle East

1930 Revolution in Ethiopia establishes Ras Tafari (1892-1975) as Emperor. He takes the name Haile Selassie.

Emperor Haile Selassie

1932 Kingdom of Saudi Arabia is established by Ibn Saud.

1932 Harry Philby, English explorer, crosses the Rub' al-Khali Desert in Arabia, known as "the Empty Quarter", probably the first European to do so.

1933 Arabs riot against Jewish immigration into Palestine. Britain limits the number allowed, to try to stop unrest.

A menorah candlestick, symbol of Judaism

1935 Italy invades Ethiopia, disobeying the terms of the League of Nations.

1935 Persia is renamed Iran.

1935 Turkish women win the vote.

1936 Anglo-Egyptian alliance ends the British protectorate over Egypt, but gives Britain control over the Suez Canal for 20 years. British troops garrison the Suez Canal zone.

1936 Italian troops capture Addis Ababa, capital of Ethiopia, and annex the country. Haile Selassie appeals for League of Nations support. Britain and France agree to impose limited sanctions on Italy.

1936 Arab revolt in Palestine against Jewish immigrants, in an attempt to stop the establishment of the state of Israel.

1938 Mussolini declares Libya part of Italy.

A map of mandated territories in the Middle East

French mandate

British mandate

Political mandate for League of Nations

GREECE TURKEY CRETE CYPRUS SYRIA PERSIA Mediterranean Sea LEBANON IRAQ PALESTINE TRANS-JORDAN LIBYA EGYPT SAUDI ARABIA Red Sea

THE SECOND WORLD WAR

In **September 1939**, Hitler invaded Poland, and Britain and France ("the Allies") declared war. By **June 1940**, Germany had occupied much of northern Europe. They moved tanks and planes with incredible speed, using a technique known as *Blitzkrieg* ("lightning war"). Between **1940** and **1941**, its airforce, the *Luftwaffe*, attacked British airports, factories and cities (the *Blitz*). In **1941**, the Germans launched operation "Barbarossa": a massive invasion of the Soviet Union, their former ally. A huge mistake, it drained German resources and forced them to retreat. In **1942**, the U.S.A. joined the Allies, after Germany's new ally, Japan, attacked Pearl Harbor in Hawaii. The Japanese won control of much of Southeast Asia and the Pacific. But, from **1942**, there were Allied victories in the Pacific and in North Africa, and in **June 1944**, the Allies landed in Normandy (D-Day). Meanwhile, the Soviets were pushing the Germans back from the East, and met the Allies in Berlin in **April 1945**. Hitler, facing inevitable defeat, committed suicide. In **May 1945**, Germany surrendered (VE day) followed in September by Japan (VJ day).

Asia

1931 Mohandas Gandhi marches 380km (238 miles) across India, in protest against British taxes.

Gandhi

1931 Mao Zedong proclaims a Chinese Soviet Republic in the remote Jiangxi province.

1931 Japanese occupy Manchuria. In 1932, they set up Republic of Manchukuo, with Chinese ex-emperor Pu Yi as President.

Map showing the Japanese invasion of China

1934 Rapid military and naval rearmament begins in Japan.

1934-1935 The Long March to northern China by Chinese Communists led by Mao Zedong. Driven from their stronghold in Jiangxi by Jiang Jie Shi, they are forced to make a 8,000km (5,000 mile) journey to Yenan, a mountainous region in northwest China. They set up government and plot to take over the whole country.

The Communist Long March of 1934-1935, led by Mao Zedong

1937 Burma is separated from British India and ruled as an individual colony.

1937-1945 The Japanese attack China. They take Shanghai and Nanking (1937), Canton and Hankow (1938).

America and Australasia

1930 Amy Johnson, English aviator, flies from London to Darwin, Australia, becoming the first woman to fly solo across the world.

Amy Johnson's plane

1930 Getulio Vargas seizes power in Brazil and becomes President.

Peruvian textiles and bowl

1932 War between Peru and Colombia.

1932 Sydney Bridge opens in Australia.

1932 The Empire State Building, the world's tallest building, is opened in New York.

1932-1935 War between Paraguay and Bolivia over disputed Chaco region.

1933 Sanchez Cherro is elected President of Peru, and assassinated by a member of the opposition.

1932-1945 F. D. Roosevelt is U.S. President. He introduces New Deal policies to deal with the Depression. The end of Prohibition.

mid 1930s Fierce winds in the U.S. plains destroy farms and wreck the landscape. The area, and the period, become known as "the Dust Bowl".

1935 Mackenzie King becomes Prime Minister of Canada.

1936 Jesse Owens, an African American, wins four gold medals at the Berlin Olympics.

U.S. and German (Nazi period) flags, and a stopwatch used at the Olympics

1938 Unsuccessful Nazi plots in Chile and Brazil.

1938-1945 Getulio Vargas is dictator of Brazil.

1939 Igor Sikorsky, a Russian-born American, designs the first modern helicopter.

Europe

1940 Battle of Britain: British win air battle with Germany.

1940 Germans occupy France. De Gaulle sets up Free French Forces (FFL) to continue fighting.

British plane

1940-1945 Sir Winston Churchill leads coalition government in Britain.

1941 Operation Barbarossa: Germans invade U.S.S.R.

1941 Frank Whittle, inventor of aircraft jet engine, flies the first British jet aircraft.

1941-1945 Nazis build concentration camps in German-occupied countries and murder over 12 million: homosexuals, mentally ill, gypsies and over six million Jews. This is known as "the Holocaust".

1942 Wernher von Braun, German scientist, launches the V-2, the first long-range jet rocket.

1943 The first electronic computer, Colossus I, is built in U.K.

1943 Italy surrenders. Germans occupy North Italy and Rome.

1944 Allies advance on all fronts. France is liberated on June 6 (D-Day). De Gaulle sets up a government in Paris in August.

1944-1949 Civil war in Greece.

1945 French women are given the vote for the first time.

1945 Hitler commits suicide. Germany surrenders on May 8 (VE Day) and splits into French, British, U.S., and Soviet zones.

Churchill, Roosevelt and Stalin, the leaders of Britain, USA and USSR, meeting at Yalta, on the Black Sea, to make plans for a postwar settlement

1945-1946 Trials of Nazi leaders at Nuremburg, Germany.

1946 Hungary, Albania and Bulgaria become republics.

1946 King of Italy abdicates and a republic is proclaimed. Italian women are given the vote for the first time.

1947 Belgium, Netherlands and Luxembourg form a Customs Union: the start of the movement for European unity.

1947 Romania becomes a republic.

1948 Communists seize power in Czechoslovakia, Hungary, Romania, Bulgaria and Poland.

1947-1958 Fourth Republic in France.

1948 Organization for European Economic Cooperation (OEEC) is established.

1948-1949 Berlin Blockade: U.S.S.R. cuts off West Berlin in an attempt to force it to join the Eastern bloc. Blockade is broken by an Anglo-American airlift of supplies. East and West Germany are established as separate states.

1949 U.K. Labour government begins nationalization policy.

1949 Eire leaves the British Commonwealth. *Irish flag*

Africa and the Middle East

Axis territory before September 1 1939
Axis satellites
Neutral countries
Allied countries
Allied occupied countries
Axis occupied countries

NORWAY SWEDEN FINLAND
ESTONIA
EIRE DENMARK LATVIA
BRITAIN LITHUANIA EAST PRUSSIA
HOLLAND GERMANY POLAND
BELGIUM
FRANCE AUSTRIA SLOVAKIA U.S.S.R.
SWITZERLAND HUNGARY BESSARABIA
PORTUGAL ROMANIA
SPAIN ITALY YUGOSLAVIA
BULGARIA
SPANISH MOROCCO ALBANIA
GREECE TURKEY
MOROCCO ALGERIA SYRIA
TUNISIA LEBANON IRAQ
LIBYA PALESTINE TRANSJORDAN

Map showing the two sides across Europe, North Africa and the Middle East during the war

1940 Italians invade Egypt, but are driven back by British, who occupy Libya.

1940 Many French African colonies support General de Gaulle's Free French Forces.

1941 General Erwin Rommel leads a German counterattack against the Allies in North Africa.

1941 Italians expelled from Somalia, Eritrea and Ethiopia.

1942 Rommel is defeated by British under General Montgomery at El Alamein, Egypt.

Rommel's troops after capture in 1941

1943 Germans surrender in Tunisia: the end of German involvement in Africa.

1945 Formation of the Arab League in Cairo.

1945 Uprising against the French in Algeria.

1946 Transjordan wins independence under King Abdullah, and is renamed Jordan.

1947 Partition of Palestine into Arab and Jewish states agreed by UN, but opposed by Arabs. Fighting breaks out after the British withdraw.

Map of Israel and Palestine 1947 - 1948

Jewish areas 1947
Arab areas 1947
Israel's border 1948

LEBANON
SYRIA
• Jerusalem
Dead Sea
PALESTINE
JORDAN
SINAI PENINSULA
SAUDI ARABIA

1948 Nationalist Party is elected in South Africa on a policy of *apartheid* (separate development for blacks and whites). Apartheid is introduced in 1949.

1948-1949 Arab League goes to war with Israel, but fails to stop the establishment of the state.

Palestinian refugees leaving Israel

Asia

1940 Friendship treaty between Siam and Japan.

1941 Neutrality pact between Soviet Union and Japan.

1941-1942 Japanese occupy much of Southeast Asia and the islands of the Pacific.

1942 Battle of Midway: U.S. halts Japanese expansion.

1944 U.S. seizes Saigon, Vietnam, and launches bombing raids against Japan.

1945 U.S. destroys Japanese fleet at Okinawa and drops atomic bombs on Japan. Hiroshima and Nagasaki are completely destroyed. Japanese surrender on August 14.

This atomic bomb, named "Fat Boy", was dropped on Nagasaki, Japan.

Inside the bomb was a substance called plutonium. Upon hitting the target, all the plutonium atoms in the bomb split, releasing huge amounts of energy.

1945 U.S.S.R. and U.S.A. jointly administer Korea.

1945 Ho Chi Minh forms a government in Hanoi, Vietnam. French attempts to reassert control lead to a war of independence in Indochina (1946-1954).

1945-1951 Allies occupy and administer Japan.

1946-1949 Civil war between nationalists and communists in China leads to communist victory. Nationalists set up state of Nationalist China in Taiwan.

1947 India is granted independence and divided into Hindu India and Muslim Pakistan. Massacres take place as people migrate to different parts of the subcontinent.

People migrating to different parts of India

1948 Mahatma Gandhi is assassinated.

1948 Terrorism leads to a state of emergency in Malaya.

1948 Two republics in Korea: a pro-communist regime in North Korea and a pro-western regime in South Korea.

1948 Burma and Ceylon are granted independence from Britain.

1949 Siam is renamed Thailand.

1949 Japan: the U.S. launches a scheme to improve the Japanese economy.

1949 Chairman Mao Zedong formally declares the communist People's Republic of China.

America and Australasia

1941 Japanese attack U.S. naval base at Pearl Harbor, Hawaii. U.S.A. enters Second World War.

The Japanese attack on Pearl Harbor

1942 First nuclear reactor is built by Enrico Fermi in U.S.A.

1942 Mexico and Brazil declare war on Germany and Japan.

1943 Revolution in Argentina: Juan Perón rises to power as virtual military dictator. He becomes President in 1946.

1945 U.S. explodes first atom bomb in New Mexico.

1945 United Nations (UN) is set up in San Francisco, U.S.A. to encourage peace and protect human rights.

UN symbol

1946 ENIAC, an early modern computer, is developed by John Mauchly and John Eckert.

1946 U.S. conducts the first underwater atomic explosion at Bikini Atoll in the Pacific.

1947 U.S. introduces the Marshall Plan, to give economic aid to non-communist countries.

German poster advertising the Marshall Plan

1947 U.S. President Harry Truman offers to support groups fighting communism.

THE COLD WAR

After World War Two, the two superpowers, the U.S.S.R. and the U.S.A., were driven apart by political differences and mutual suspicion. Both sides built up nuclear forces and engaged in a war of propaganda and threats. Although there was no direct fighting between them, the two sides supported armed struggles between communists and non-communists in other parts of the world. This state of hostility was known as the Cold War, and lasted from 1948 until the dissolution of the Soviet Union in 1991.

1948 Invention of the transistor miniaturizes electronic circuitry.

1949 North Atlantic Treaty Organization (NATO) is formed: a military alliance to counter the communist threat.

Europe

1951 U.S.S.R. explodes its first atom bomb.

1951 European Coal and Steel Treaty between Belgium, France, Holland, Italy, Luxembourg and West Germany.

1952 Elizabeth II becomes Queen of Great Britain and Northern Ireland.

1953 DNA structure is discovered by Francis Crick (U.K.) and James Watson (U.S.).

The double helix shape of a DNA molecule

1953 U.S.S.R.: Death of Stalin. Nikita Khrushchev becomes first secretary, then premier (1958-1964).

1953 Imre Nagy, liberal Communist Party leader, introduces reforms in Hungary.

1953 Josip Broz, known as Tito, is elected President of Yugoslavia.

1953 Soviet tanks crush anti-communist uprising in East Berlin.

1954 Roger Bannister (U.K.) runs first four-minute mile.

1954 EOKA movement in Cyprus struggles for union with Greece. Anti-British unrest until 1959.

1955 The Warsaw Pact is signed: a military treaty and association between the communist states of Eastern Europe.

Map of divided Europe

1956 Anti-communist uprising in Hungary is crushed by the U.S.S.R. Imre Nagy is executed in 1958.

Soviet tanks putting down the anti-communist revolt in Hungary in 1956

1957 U.S.S.R. launches the first Space satellite, *Sputnik 1*. Laika, a small dog, becomes first living creature in Space.

1957 Treaty of Rome establishes the European Economic Community (EEC). Members: France, Germany, Italy, Belgium, Netherlands and Luxembourg.

1958 De Gaulle becomes Prime Minister, then President, of France (1959-1969). The Fifth Republic is established.

1959 The first air cushioned vehicle (ACV), designed by Christopher Cockerell (U.K.), makes first sea crossing.

1959 Archbishop Makarios becomes first president of new republic of Cyprus.

Africa and the Middle East

1951 Libya becomes first African colony to win independence.

1951 King Abdullah of Jordan is assassinated. Crown Prince Hussein becomes King of Jordan.

1952 Revolution in Egypt: King Farouk abdicates. A republic is proclaimed in 1953.

1952-1955 State of emergency in Kenya: uprisings by Mau Mau, a secret society opposed to British rule.

Kenyan shields

1953 Federation of North and South Rhodesia and Nyasaland is established.

1954 Gamal Abdul Nasser comes to power in Egypt. He is President from 1956-1970.

1954-1962 Bitter civil war between Algerian nationalists and French settlers leads to independence.

1956 Second Arab-Israeli War.

1956 Oil is discovered in Nigeria.

1956 Sudan and Morocco become independent.

1956 Suez Crisis: President Nasser of Egypt nationalizes the Suez Canal, opposed by Britain and France. Israel invades Egypt, and Britain and France occupy the Canal Zone. U.S. opposition and world opinion force them to withdraw.

1957 Tunisia becomes a republic.

1957 King Feisal II and Iraqi Prime Minister are assassinated in an army coup. Republic proclaimed.

1957 Gold Coast (renamed Ghana) becomes independent under Kwame Nkrumah. Major step in the decolonization of Africa.

Ghanaian flag

1958 Egypt and Syria form United Arab Republic (U.A.R.), later joined by Yemen. Syria leaves in 1960.

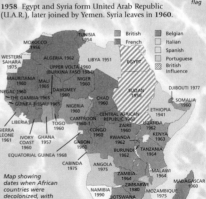

Map showing dates when African countries were decolonized, with their new names

Asia

Map of Korea in 1953

U.S. tank from the Korean war

1950-1953
The Korean War: North Korea, backed by the U.S.S.R., invades South Korea. UN forces (mainly U.S.) support South Korea. China supports North Korea. Communists make gains at first, but in 1951 UN forces counterattack. Treaty of Panmunjon (1953) establishes the border between North and South Korea.

1950 China invades Tibet.

1951 Mussadeq, Prime Minister of Iran, nationalizes the Anglo-Iranian Oil Company. Tension with Britain follows.

1951 1952 Postwar peace treaty gives full independence to Japan. Rapid economic growth begins. U.S. occupation ends.

1953 Edmund Hillary (N.Z.) and Sherpa Tensing (Nepal) reach the summit of Everest, the world's highest mountain.

The world's highest mountains

Everest, Himalayas 8,846m(29,022ft)	K2, Himalayas
Mont Blanc, Alps	McKinley, Alaska Range	Aconcagua, Andes
Fujiyama, Japan	Kilimanjaro, East Africa

1954 Southeast Asia Treaty Organization (SEATO) is set up by Australia, France, New Zealand, U.K., Pakistan, Philippines, Thailand and U.S.A. to check the spread of communism.

1957 Malaya wins independence.

THE VIETNAM WAR

Map of Indochina 1953

The struggle for independence in Indochina ended with the French defeat at Dien Bien Phu in 1954. North Vietnam set up an independent communist state, based in Hanoi. The same year, at a conference in Geneva, Cambodia, Laos and South Vietnam were recognized as independent states. But North Vietnam refused to accept the division of Vietnam, and civil war broke out (1954-1973). The North supported the Viet Cong, southern rebels who wanted to join them, while the U.S. supported the South Vietnam government. From 1961, the Americans became actively involved, bombing the north from 1965. Despite a huge U.S. presence (half a million troops by 1968), the Viet Cong were masters of jungle warfare. In 1973, with demoralized troops and hostility to the war at home, the Americans withdrew. By 1975, the Viet Cong had taken the southern capital, Saigon (now Ho Chi Minh city), and united the country.

1958 China: Mao Zedong announces the Great Leap Forward, a plan for rapid industrial growth.

1959 Unsuccessful uprising in Tibet against the Chinese. The Dalai Lama flees to India.

America and Australasia

1950 Death of Eva Perón, popular and influential wife of President Juan Perón of Argentina.

1950 U.S. President Truman allows development of hydrogen bomb.

American poster warning of the dangers of communism

1950-1954 Senator McCarthy leads drive against communism in U.S.A.

1951 Australia, New Zealand and U.S.A. sign ANZUS pact.

1952 Civil war in Cuba: General Batista seizes power, opposed by communists led by Fidel Castro.

1954 First inoculations against polio in the U.S.

1955 Revolution in Argentina overthrows Juan Perón.

1955 Martin Luther King leads a boycott of buses in Alabama, U.S.A., in an attempt to end segregation.

1958 Integrated circuit, or silicon chip, is demonstrated by Jack Kilby of Texas Instruments, U.S.A.

The silicon chip (right) miniaturizes electronic circuitry.

 1958 Alaska becomes 49th state of U.S.A.

1958-1967 Growing demands for civil rights for African Americans in U.S.A.

1959 Failed invasion of Cuba by a small band of Cuban exiles trained by the American C.I.A

 1959 Hawaii becomes 50th state of U.S.A.

The number of stars on the American flag, known as the Stars and Stripes, equals the number of states in the union.

1959 Cuba: Fidel Castro overthrows President Batista, with the help of Che Guevara, an Argentinian Marxist experienced in guerilla warfare.

Images of Che Guevara became a symbol of revolution all over the world.

Europe

1960 Cyprus becomes independent.

1961 Yuri Gagarin (U.S.S.R.) makes first manned spaceflight. He completes an entire orbit of the Earth in *Vostok 1*.

1961 Berlin Wall is built around East Berlin, to stop East Germans from fleeing to the West.

The Berlin Wall by the Brandenburg Gate

Soviet tank patrolling the border zone

1961 Amnesty International is founded in London, to fight for human rights.

1962 U.K. application to join EEC is rejected.

1963 Valentina Tereshkova (U.S.S.R.) is first woman in space.

Valentina in the command module of Vostok 6

1963 U.S.S.R., U.K. and U.S.A. sign Nuclear Test Ban Treaty.

1964 Fighting between Greeks and Turks in Cyprus.

1964 Leonid Brezhnev succeeds Khrushchev as Soviet leader.

1965 Sir Winston Churchill, British wartime leader, dies.

1965 Alexei Leonov (U.S.S.R.) is first to "walk in space".

1967 Greek monarchy is abolished.

MAY '68

In **May 1968**, student demonstrations broke out in Paris against university conditions and other issues, including U.S. involvement in the Vietnam War, and quickly spread to other parts of France. Revolution was in the air, as suppression by the police led to violent clashes between riot police and up to 30,000 students. Workers joined forces with the students, ending in a general strike against President de Gaulle's policies. He resigned as President in **1969**.

October 1968 Soviet troops invade Czechoslovakia to crush the "Prague Spring", a liberal movement in the Czech Communist Party, led by Prime Minister Alexander Dubcek.

1968-1969 Civil rights riots in Northern Ireland. Period of violence and clashes between Unionists (who want to keep union with Britain) and Republicans (who want separation).

Africa and the Middle East

1960s Most African countries become independent.

Flags of Uganda (1962), Botswana (1966), Ghana (1957), Swaziland (1968) and Togo (1960)

1960 Organization of Petroleum Exporting Countries (OPEC) is set up in Baghdad, Iraq.

1960 Sharpeville massacre in South Africa. 67 black Africans are killed when troops fire on a demonstration.

1960-1965 Civil war in the Congo following independence from Belgium. A military coup brings President Mobutu to power. Katanga province declares independence.

1961 South Africa leaves the Commonwealth.

1962 Revolution in Yemen. The monarchy is abolished.

1963 Organization for African Unity (OAU) is formed in Addis Ababa, Ethiopia, by 30 African countries.

1963 Kenya becomes independent under Prime Minister Jomo Kenyatta. It becomes a republic in **1964**.

1964 Tanganyika and Zanzibar unite to become Tanzania.

1964 Rebel activity against the Portuguese in Mozambique.

1964 Last French forces leave Algeria.

1965 Ian Smith, Rhodesian Front Party leader, declares Southern Rhodesia independent under white minority rule. This is known as the Unilateral Declaration of Independence, or UDI. Britain does not accept it and imposes sanctions. Long civil war follows, as black guerillas fight for power.

Emblem used on Bokassa's robe

1966 Jean Bokassa seizes power in Central African Republic.

1966 Milton Obote seizes power in Uganda.

1966 Nkrumah is overthrown in Ghana by military coup.

1966 South African Prime Minister Verwoerd is assassinated.

1966 Revolution in Nigeria.

1967 Six Days' War between Israel and Arab states. Israel occupies Sinai.

1967 First successful heart transplant performed in South Africa by Dr. Christiaan Barnard.

1967-1970 Nigerian Civil War: Eastern Nigeria breaks away and declares independence as Biafra.

1969 Revolution in Libya overthrows King Idris I and puts Colonel Gadaffi in power.

1969 Golda Meir becomes Prime Minister of Israel.

Asia

1960 War between China and India over disputed border.

1960 Worsening relations between China and U.S.S.R.

1960 Mrs. Bandaranaike of Sri Lanka becomes first elected woman prime minister.

1961 U.S. starts sending troops to South Vietnam, to fight attacks by communist North Vietnamese, the Vietminh. They begin bombing North Vietnam in 1965.

1961 Death of Jawaharlal Nehru, popular Prime Minister of India since independence in 1947.

1964 State of emergency in Malaya after attacks by Indonesian guerillas.

1965 U.S. sends first ground troops into Vietnam.

1965 India and Pakistan fight over the Kashmir region on the border between them.

1965 Singapore becomes independent from Malaya.

1965 Ferdinand Marcos becomes President of Philippines.

1966 Indira Gandhi becomes Prime Minister of India.

THE CULTURAL REVOLUTION

In 1966, the Chinese leader, Mao Zedong, launched the Cultural Revolution: a period of terror during which supposed capitalist influences were crushed, in an attempt to keep to pure communist ideals. Young people were encouraged to join the Red Guards, who used spying, violence and intimidation to seek out anti-revolutionaries. This lasted until Mao's death in 1976, and millions of people were killed or imprisoned.

Chinese flag

Support for Mao during the Cultural Revolution

1967 China explodes its first hydrogen bomb.

1968 Tet offensive: North Vietnam launches a major campaign against South Vietnam. Peace negotiations begin.

U.S. helicopter over a Vietnamese village

America and Australasia

1960 New city of Brasilia becomes the new capital of Brazil.

1961 Bay of Pigs: an invasion of Cuba, backed by the U.S.A. to overthrow Fidel Castro, fails.

1962 Jamaica, Trinidad and Tobago gain independence.

1962 The U.S. launches Telstar, the first satellite to relay live television and telephone calls.

Telstar satellite

THE CUBAN MISSILE CRISIS

In 1962 came the most dangerous moment of the Cold War, as the world teetered for days on the brink of nuclear war. The U.S.A. discovered that the Soviet Union had established nuclear bases in Cuba. Seeing its security at risk, the U.S. began a naval blockade of the island, threatening war unless the bases were dismantled. Eventually, however, the U.S.S.R. was persuaded to back down.

1963 U.S. President Kennedy is assassinated in Dallas, Texas.

1963 Viking remains are found in North America dating back 500 years before Christopher Columbus.

1964 President Johnson signs U.S. Civil Rights Bill, outlawing racial discrimination.

1965 First U.S. spacecraft lands on the Moon.

1965 Malcolm X, African American militant leader, is assassinated in New York.

1966 British Guiana (Guyana) and Barbados become independent.

1967 Che Guevara, leader of guerillas in Bolivia, is assassinated.

1968 Martin Luther King, an African American civil rights leader, is assassinated.

1968 Pierre Trudeau becomes Prime Minister of Canada.

1968 U.S. Senator Robert F. Kennedy is assassinated.

1969 Anti Vietnam War demonstrations grow.

An anti war poster

1969 Half a million attend a rock festival at Woodstock, U.S.A.

1969 July 21: U.S. astronaut Neil Armstrong is the first man on the Moon.

'One small step' for Neil Armstrong

Europe

1970 First jumbo jet lands in London from New York.

1970 British find oil in North Sea.

An offshore oil rig

1970 Death of President de Gaulle of France.

1970 Spain: serious unrest among Basque separatists (people from the Basque region who want separation from Spain).

1971 Former Soviet leader Nikita Khrushchev dies.

1971 Decimal currency is adopted in Britain.

1971 Women are given the vote in Switzerland.

1971 U.S.S.R. launches the world's first space station, *Salyut 1*.

1972 Munich Olympic Games: Israeli athletes are murdered by *Black September*, an Arab terrorist organization.

The Olympic logo

1972 Bloody Sunday in northern Ireland. Troops fire on rioters, killing 13. Britain imposes direct rule.

1973 Eire, Denmark and U.K. join the EEC.

1973 Greece becomes a republic. President Papadopoulos is overthrown in a military coup.

1974 Turks invade Cyprus and split the island into northern Turkish sector and southern Greek sector.

1974 Revolution in Portugal. The military dictatorship is overthrown and replaced by democracy.

1975 Death of General Franco in Spain. The monarchy is restored under King Juan Carlos.

1975 West Germany: trial of Baader-Meinhof terrorist gang.

1976 Helsinki Convention on Human Rights is adopted.

Concorde creates a supersonic bang as it passes the speed of sound.

1976 Concorde, the world's first supersonic (faster than the speed of sound) passenger plane, designed by Britain and France, begins a service flying across the Atlantic.

1977 King Juan Carlos restores democracy in Spain.

1977 *Charter 77*, a human rights organization, is formed, led by Czech playwright Vaclav Havel.

1978 First test-tube baby, Louise Brown, born in U.K.

1978 World's worst oil spill: tanker *Amoco Cadiz* runs aground off French coast losing 1.3 million barrels of oil.

1979 Lord Mountbatten is killed by an IRA bomb.

1979 Margaret Thatcher becomes the first woman prime minister in U.K.

Africa and the Middle East

1970 King Hussein of Jordan and Yasser Arafat of the PLO (Palestine Liberation Organization) sign a truce to end the war in Jordan.

1970 Military coup in Uganda brings Idi Amin to power.

1970 Israel and Egypt fight over Sinai.

Israeli F4E fighter plane

1971 Aswan Dam is opened in Egypt.

1972 Idi Amin expels over 40,000 Asians living in Uganda.

1973 Yom Kippur War between Israel and Arab states. Egypt and Syria attack Israel and occupy Golan Heights. OPEC restricts oil supplies: this leads to huge increases in oil prices and a worldwide economic crisis.

This oil 'supertanker' is so long that crew members need a moped to ride from one end to the other.

1974 Haile Selassie is deposed and a Marxist government is established in Ethiopia.

1974 Civil war begins between rival religious (Christian and Muslim) and political groups in Lebanon.

1975 Angola and Mozambique become independent. Civil war begins in Angola.

1975 King Faisal of Saudi Arabia is assassinated.

1976 Serious rioting in Soweto, near Johannesburg.

1976 Raid on Entebbe: Israeli commandos free 100 hostages held by Palestinian terrorists at Entebbe, Uganda.

1977 Jean Bokassa crowns himself emperor of the Central African Empire.

1977 President Sadat of Egypt visits Israel for peace talks.

1978 UN peace troops sent to Israel/Lebanon border.

Map of Lebanon, showing the majority religious group in each area

Sunni
Shia
Druze
Christian
Israeli security zone

LEBANON
Tripoli
Beirut
Baalbek
Sidon
Tyre
SYRIA
ISRAEL

1979 Peace treaty between Israel and Egypt. Israel agrees to withdraw from Sinai.

1979 Shah of Iran is overthrown, and an Islamic republic is set up, led by Ayatollah Khomeini.

1979 Uganda: civil war and military invasion by Tanzania leads to the overthrow of Idi Amin.

1979 Lancaster House Conference in London draws up a constitution for majority rule in Rhodesia, to be renamed Zimbabwe.

Zimbabwe flag

Asia

1970 Military coup in Cambodia overthrows the government of Prince Sihanouk. Khmer Republic is set up by Lon Nol.

1971 Pakistan attacks India, but is defeated.

1971 Pakistan is forced to give up East Pakistan, which forms the independent state of Bangladesh.

The flag of Bangladesh

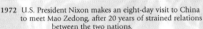

1972 Ceylon changes its name to Sri Lanka.

1972 U.S. President Nixon makes an eight-day visit to China to meet Mao Zedong, after 20 years of strained relations between the two nations.

1973 Ceasefire in Vietnam: the last American troops leave.

1973 The King of Afghanistan is overthrown in a military coup. Muhammad Daoud reasserts control.

1974 Largest ever tomb is discovered, belonging to Chinese emperor Shi Huangdi.

The tomb of Emperor Shi Huangdi contained a terracotta army of over 7,500 soldiers, horses and chariots.

1975 North and South Vietnam are united under communist rule.

1975 Communists seize power in Cambodia and Laos. Khmer Rouge, Cambodian communists, are led by dictator Pol Pot. Millions die under his rule.

1976 China: Mao Zedong dies. Fall from power of the "Gang of Four", Mao's closest associates, including his widow.

1977 Thousands of Vietnamese people leave in boats, fleeing the communist regime in South Vietnam.

1977 Military coup in Pakistan by General Zia al-Haq. Former President Bhutto is overthrown and later hanged.

1978 Vietnamese invade Cambodia to help rebels overthrow Khmer Rouge government. A pro-Vietnamese regime is set up.

1979 Civil war against the pro-Soviet regime in Afghanistan. Soviet troops invade in support of the government. Guerilla war follows.

1979 The Killing Fields: huge graves are found in Cambodia, evidence of mass murder under Pol Pot's regime.

America and Australasia

1970 U.S. national guardsmen shoot four students dead at a demonstration at Kent State University, Ohio.

1971 Death of François "Papa Doc" Duvalier, President of Haiti since 1957. He is succeeded by his son Jean-Claude "Baby Doc".

1972 U.S.A. and U.S.S.R. sign SALT (Strategic Arms Limitation Treaty) to reduce the number of missiles.

1973 Australia: opening of the Sydney Opera House.

1973 U.S.-backed military coup in Chile, led by General Pinochet. Marxist President Allende is killed.

Chilean flag

1973 Juan Perón becomes President of Argentina again.

1973 Civil war in Nicaragua, between the *Sandinistas* (nationalist and communist guerillas) and the government (ruled by the Somoza family since 1933).

1974 Isabel Perón becomes President of Argentina, after the death of her husband, Juan Perón. She is deposed in 1976.

1973-1974 Watergate scandal in U.S.A.: bugging devices found in Democrat election campaign headquarters. President Nixon faces impeachment by Congress and resigns.

1975 Altair, the first personal computer, is sold in the U.S.A.

1975 First international meeting in space: Soviet and U.S. spacecraft dock together and astronauts shake hands through the hatches.

1975 Constitutional crisis in Australia after Labour Prime Minister Gough Whitlam is dismissed.

1977 Space shuttle, the first reusable spacecraft, is tested.

The first Space shuttle was named 'Enterprise' after the spaceship in the popular TV series Star Trek.

1978 Camp David Agreement between Israel and Egypt.

1978 U.S. begins diplomatic relations with China.

1978 900 members of a religious cult die in a mass suicide in Guyana.

1979 Nicaragua: Somoza is overthrown. Sandinista government comes to power.

1979 Three mile island: worst nuclear leak in U.S. history.

The radioactive symbol

Europe

1980 Death of President Tito, ruler in Yugoslavia since 1945.

Solidarity logo

1980 Unrest in Poland, as independent trade union *Solidarnosc* (Solidarity), led by Lech Walesa, wins support. Government declares martial law, bans Solidarity, and imprisons many of its leaders.

1980 Terrorist bomb kills 84 at Bologna railway station, Italy.

1981 François Mitterand is first Socialist President of France.

1981 United Kingdom: Charles, Prince of Wales marries Lady Diana Spencer.

1981 Greece joins the EEC.

1982 AIDS virus is identified in France.

Model of the AIDS virus

1984 U.K.: IRA bomb hits Conservative Conference.

1984-1985 Irish singer Bob Geldof organizes Band Aid and Live Aid, raising millions for Ethiopia.

1985 Mikhail Gorbachev becomes leader in the U.S.S.R.

1985 Talks between Reagan and Gorbachev in Geneva.

1986 Reykjavik talks between Reagan and Gorbachev fail.

1986 Major nuclear power disaster at Chernobyl, U.S.S.R.

1986 Spain and Portugal join EEC.

1987 Hurricane hits southern Britain and northern France.

1987 Gorbachev encourages *glasnost* ("openness") and *perestroika* ("restructuring") in the U.S.S.R.

1988 Plane crashes in Lockerbie, Scotland, killing all 259 passengers and crew, after terrorist bomb explodes on board.

1988 Communist government is forced to resign in Czechoslovakia after peaceful pro-democracy demonstrations. Vaclav Havel is elected President.

1988 Strikes by Polish union Solidarity bring the economy to a standstill and the government is forced to hold talks.

1989 British writer Salman Rushdie is condemned to death by Ayatollah Khomeini for his book *The Satanic Verses*.

1989 Tim Berners-Lee, British scientist, invents World Wide Web.

1989 Hungary opens border with Austria, allowing the free flow of people from East to West for the first time.

1989 Pro-democracy demonstrations all over Germany: The government gives in and the Berlin Wall is knocked down.

Berliners celebrating the opening up of the wall

1989 Civil war in Romania. President Ceausescu is executed.

1989 Tadeusz Mazowiecki is elected Prime Minister of a Solidarity-led government in Poland.

Africa and the Middle East

1980 Rhodesia becomes independent as Zimbabwe, with Robert Mugabe as Prime Minister.

1980 War breaks out between Iran and Iraq.

1981 President Sadat of Egypt is assassinated. Hosni Mubarak is elected president.

1982 Israel invades Lebanon, in an attempt to drive out the PLO (Palestine Liberation Organization) and establish a strong Christian government in Beirut. Syria opposes Israel. Civil war follows. Hundreds of Palestinians are massacred in Shabra and Shatila refugee camps.

PLO poster

1984-1985 10-year drought and civil war lead to famine in Ethiopia, Sudan and Chad. Thousands die.

1985 War between Iran and Iraq intensifies.

Flags of Iran (top) and Iraq (bottom)

1985 Israeli troops withdraw from Lebanon.

1985 Riots in Eastern Cape, South Africa.

1986 State of Emergency declared in South Africa. Serious rioting and hundreds of deaths follow police violence.

1986 Desmond Tutu becomes first black archbishop of Cape Town, South Africa.

1986 U.S. bombs Libya, after Libyans carry out acts of terrorism in Europe.

1986 Commonwealth and U.S. agree to economic sanctions against South Africa.

1986 New constitution is adopted in Ethiopia. Colonel Mengistu Mariam becomes first president.

1987 Mohammed Barre is re-elected President of Somalia.

1988 Refugees flee to Ethiopia from Sudan.

1988 South Africa signs peace agreement with Angola and Cuba.

1988 Refugees flee to Rwanda after massacres in Burundi.

1988 Yasser Arafat, PLO leader, renounces terrorism and recognizes right of Israel to exist.

1989 F. W. de Klerk becomes President of South Africa.

1989 Death of Iranian leader, Ayatollah Khomeini.

Mourners at Khomeini's funeral

Asia

1982 First compact disc (CD) introduced by Sony (Japan) and Phillips (Holland).

Compact disc

1983 Unrest and violence between Tamil separatists and Singhalese majority in Sri Lanka.

1983 Korean Air Lines flight 007 is shot down by Soviet fighter plane, killing 269 people on board.

1983 Philippines opposition leader Benigno Aquino is assassinated.

1984 Britain and China agree on terms for the handing over of Hong Kong to China.

1984 Golden temple at Amritsar, India, is occupied by Sikh extremists demanding an independent state. Indian police storm the temple, fighting breaks out and hundreds die. Months later, Prime Minister Indira Gandhi is assassinated by a Sikh bodyguard. She is succeeded by her son, Rajiv.

1984 Chemical leak at factory in Bhopal, India, kills over 2,000 people.

1986 President Marcos is ousted after 20 years in power in the Philippines. He is succeeded by Corazon Aquino.

1987 India sends troops to Sri Lanka to control Tamil rebels.

1987 China: Chairman Deng Xiaoping resigns from all posts, except control of the army.

1988 President Zia al-Haq, military ruler of Pakistan, is killed when his plane explodes mid-air. Benazir Bhutto becomes first woman Prime Minister of Pakistan.

1988 World's longest tunnel opens between islands of Honshu and Hokkaido in Japan.

1988 Over 1,000 people die in floods in Bangladesh.

1988 Major earthquake in Armenia, killing 100,000 people.

1988 President of Burma resigns after riots and anti-government demonstrations.

1989 Soviet army completes withdrawal from Afghanistan.

1989 Death of Emperor Hirohito of Japan, the longest reigning monarch in the world.

1989 Soviet troops withdraw from Afghanistan.

1989 Chinese troops massacre peaceful pro-democracy protesters at Tiananmen Square, Beijing.

The protest at Tiananmen Square

America and Australasia

1980 Archbishop Romero is murdered in church in El Salvador.

1980 John Lennon, former member of pop group *The Beatles*, is killed by a gunman in New York.

1981 The first IBM Personal Computer (PC) is made.

1981 Ronald Reagan becomes U.S. President.

1981 The space shuttle makes its first spaceflight.

1982 British Honduras becomes independent Belize.

1982 Falklands War: Argentina invades the Falkland Islands. British naval task force retakes the islands.

1982 Scientists spot a hole in the ozone layer over Antarctica.

1983 Left-wing coup in Grenada is put down with U.S. intervention.

1983 Military regime falls and democracy is restored in Argentina.

1985 Democracy is restored in Brazil and Uruguay.

1985 U.S. supplies aid to the Contra rebels in Nicaragua.

1985 Colombian volcano erupts.

1985 French sink Greenpeace boat *Rainbow Warrior* in New Zealand. Greenpeace had been trying to stop French nuclear testing in the Pacific.

The Rainbow Warrior, and a blue whale, one of the endangered species Greenpeace is trying to protect

1986 *Voyager 2* sends pictures of Uranus.

1986 *Challenger* space shuttle explodes on liftoff, killing all seven astronauts.

1986 U.S. Iran-Contra scandal.

1987 Washington treaty eliminates medium range nuclear missiles.

1987 Stock Market crash begins in New York.

1988 Australia celebrates 200th anniversary of first settlers from Britain.

1989 Stealth bomber B-2 developed by Northrop and U.S. air force.

1989 U.S. invades Panama. Dictator Noriega is removed from power.

1989 Oil tanker *Exxon Valdez* runs aground off Alaska, spilling thousands of barrels of crude oil.

A sea bird suffering the ill effects of the oil spill

Europe

1990 Germany is reunified.

1990 Tadeusz Mazowiecki takes up position as Prime Minister of a Solidarity-led government in Poland. Former Solidarity leader Lech Walesa is President.

1990 Boris Yeltsin is elected President of Republic of Russia.

1990 Latvia, Lithuania and Estonia claim independence.

1990 Free elections are held in Hungary, won by the non-communist Democratic Forum.

1990 Coalition government is elected in Romania.

1990 Margaret Thatcher resigns as British Prime Minister.

1990 Mary Robinson becomes the first woman President of Eire.

1991 Soviet leader, Mikhail Gorbachev, is ousted in a coup led by military and KGB leaders. Gorbachev is restored, but later resigns. U.S.S.R. is dissolved, and renamed the Commonwealth of Independent States (C.I.S.).

Flags of the old Soviet Union (U.S.S.R.) and the new Commonwealth of Independent States (Russia)

Soviet peace poster

1991 Latvia, Lithuania and Estonia become independent.

1991 Civil war breaks out in Yugoslavia. Croatia, Macedonia and Slovenia declare independence.

1992 Bosnia-Herzegovina becomes independent.

1993 Czechoslovakia splits into Czech and Slovak republics.

1993 Single European Market is established.

1993 Downing Street Declaration: British and Irish prime ministers work for peace in northern Ireland.

1994 Channel Tunnel opens between Britain and France.

Digging the Channel Tunnel

1994-1996 IRA (Irish Republican Army) ceasefire.

1994 Ferry *Estonia* sinks in the Baltic Sea. Over 900 drowned.

1994 Russian tanks invade breakaway region of Chechenia, which is demanding independence from Russia.

1995 End of fighting in Bosnia between Bosnian Serbs and government forces.

1995 Scientists in Geneva create antimatter for the first time.

1995 Austria, Finland and Sweden join the EU.

1995 Jacques Chirac is elected President of France.

1995 London: collapse of Barings Bank, after trader Nick Leeson makes huge losses in Singapore.

Africa and the Middle East

1990 Rwanda invaded by Tutsi-led rebels. The invasion is contained, and multiparty democracy is established.

1990 Namibia becomes independent from South Africa.

1990 Worldwide ban on ivory trade is introduced to protect elephants from dying out.

1990 Iraqi leader Saddam Hussein, invades Kuwait. Leads to worldwide protest and a rise in oil prices.

1990 ANC (African National Congress) ban is lifted in South Africa. *Apartheid* begins to break up. Nelson Mandela is released after 27 years in prison.

1990-1991 Gulf War: UN operation "Desert Storm" forces Iraq to withdraw from Kuwait. Iraqi forces leak two million barrels of oil into the Persian Gulf, causing the worst oil pollution in history.

1991 Mogadishu, Somali capital, is captured by rebel forces and President Barre is overthrown.

1991 Famine in Sudan.

1992-1995 UN peacekeepers fail to keep peace in Somalia.

1992 Civil war in Algeria. Fundamentalist Islamic Salvation Front wins control of local government.

1993 Peace agreement between Yasser Arafat, PLO leader, and Israeli Prime Minister Yitzhak Rabin. Some self-rule for Palestinians on Gaza Strip and West Bank of River Jordan.

1993 Ethiopia recognizes Eritrea's independence.

1994 Nelson Mandela becomes the first black President of South Africa, after the first multiracial elections.

The new South African flag

Nelson Mandela

1994 Civil war in Rwanda, between Hutu people and the Tutsi government. Thousands die.

1995 Nigerian military government executes dissident writer Ken Saro-Wiwa and eight environmental campaigners.

1995 Israeli Prime Minister Yitzhak Rabin is assassinated by a Jewish extremist.

Asia

1990 Benazir Bhutto, Prime Minister of Pakistan, is dismissed by the President on charges of corruption. She is re-elected for a second term in 1993.

1991 Rajiv Gandhi, former Prime Minister of India, is murdered by a suicide bomber during an election rally near Madras.

1991 A military junta, led by General Sunthorn Kongsompong, takes power in Thailand.

1991 Cyclone in Bangladesh kills 125,000 people, leaving 10 million homeless.

Flooded Bangladeshi village

1991 Burmese opposition leader, Aung Sang Suu Kyi, under house arrest in Burma, is awarded the Nobel Peace Prize.

Aung Sang Suu Kyi

1994 Death of Kim Il Sung of North Korea, longest ruling dictator of the 20th century.

1995 Meeting of APEC (Asia-Pacific Economic Co-operation): mutual opening of markets planned for 2020.

1995 Earthquake destroys much of Kobe, Japan.

1995 Religious sect releases poison gas on trains in Tokyo, Japan, killing 10 people.

1995-1996 France carries out nuclear testing at Mururoa atoll, South Pacific.

America and Australasia

1990 Hubble Space Telescope is launched from Cape Canaveral, U.S.A, to probe the furthest reaches of the universe.

1990 Sandinista government is defeated in Nicaraguan elections by a U.S.-backed coalition.

1991 Paul Keating becomes Australian Prime Minister.

1992 Virtual Reality is developed by Gilman Louie in U.S.A.

1992 Boutros Boutros-Ghali becomes UN secretary-general.

1992 The first UN summit on the environment, to try to tackle air pollution and global warming, is held in Brazil.

Rainforest wildlife

1992 Mass riots in Los Angeles, U.S.A., after four white policemen are acquitted of beating a black motorist.

1993 Bill Clinton becomes U.S. president.

1993 Huge bomb damages World Trade Center in New York.

1993 51-day siege in Waco, Texas. 80 cult members commit suicide.

1993 Yitzak Rabin, Israeli Prime Minister, and Yasser Arafat, leader of the PLO, sign peace accord in Washington D.C.

1993 Native Titles Bill is passed in Australia. A tribunal is set up to try to restore land rights to native Aboriginals.

Aboriginal clapsticks

1994-1995 Trial of football star O.J. Simpson, for the murder of his ex-wife, is seen by millions on TV, and drags on for months.

1994 U.S. forces occupy Haiti and restore elected President Aristide to power after military coup.

1995 Bomb wrecks federal building in Oklahoma City: the worst terrorist attack in U.S. history.

1995 Quebec votes to remain part of Canada.

Quebec flag

Europe

1996 Outbreak of BSE, or "mad cow disease", in Britain leads to widespread concern. Many countries ban British beef.

1996 Ceasefire between Chechen rebels and Russian troops in Chechenia. Peace treaty signed.

1997 Dolly, first sheep cloned using the cells of adult sheep, is born in Scotland.

Sheep cloned in a laboratory

1997 Economic collapse leads to popular uprising in Albania. Government falls.

1997 U.K.: Tony Blair becomes Labour Prime Minister in landslide victory, after 18 years of Conservative rule.

Tony and Cherie Blair (and family) outside number 10 Downing Street after the 1997 election victory

1997 Diana, Princess of Wales, is killed in a car crash in Paris.

1998 Former Chilean dictator, General Pinochet, is arrested in London for human rights abuses.

1998 Good Friday Accord, between Protestant loyalists and Catholic republicans, brings fragile peace to Northern Ireland.

1998 Russia faces economic collapse.

1998 European Union agrees on a single currency, to be called the *Euro*.

1998 Civil war in Kosovo province of Yugoslavia between Serbs and ethnic Albanians.

1999 Northern Ireland becomes self-governing.

1999 Czech Republic, Poland and Hungary join NATO.

1999 NATO bombs Serbia to try to end the war in Kosovo.

1999 More than 15,600 people die in an earthquake in Turkey, and 600,000 are left homeless.

Africa and the Middle East

1996 Hardline Benjamin Netanyahu becomes Israeli Prime Minister. Middle East peace process is in doubt.

1996 U.S. bombs southern Iraq after Iraqi forces invade safe havens designated for Kurdish minority in Iraq.

1996 Ethiopian forces attack Muslim fundamentalist militia in northern Somalia.

1996 225,000 Hutus flee to Rwanda from eastern Zaire .

1997 President Mobutu of Zaire deposed. Replaced by rebel leader Laurent Kabila. Zaire renamed Democratic Republic of Congo.

1997 Israel hands back part of Hebron (and other land) to Palestinians but establishes Jewish settlement in Arab East Jerusalem. Middle East peace process at a deadlock.

1997 Atrocities in Algeria, allegedly carried out by anti-government forces.

1997 Massacre of over 60 tourists near Luxor, Egypt, allegedly by Islamic extremists.

Queen Hatshepsut's tomb, near the site of the massacre

1998 Terrorists bomb U.S. embassies in Kenya and Tanzania. U.S. launches missile strikes against Sudan and Afghanistan.

1998 Wye Mills Agreement between Israeli Prime Minister Netanyahu and P.L.O. leader Yasser Arafat.

1998 U.S.A. and U.K. launch air strikes against Iraq, after Iraq fails to allow UN weapons inspections.

1999 King Hussein of Jordan and King Hassan II of Morocco die.

1999 Peace accord between Ehud Barak, new Prime Minister in Israel, and Yasser Arafat.

1999 Nelson Mandela retires and is succeeded by Thabo Mbeki.

Asia

1996 Bombing campaign in Sri Lanka by the Tamil Tigers. State of emergency extended.

1996 Taliban Islamic fundamentalists seize Kabul, Afghanistan.

1997 Death of former Chairman Deng Xiaoping in China.

1997 Violent demonstrations in Seoul, South Korea.

1997 Fires caused by forest clearance in Indonesia grow out of control, spreading pollution through Southeast Asia.

1997 Asian economic crisis begins as Japan raises consumption tax and Thailand floats its currency.

1997 Hong Kong, 99-year lease to Britain expires on June 30. Britain returns Hong Kong to China on July 1.

Hong Kong street scene

1998 India and Pakistan both conduct atomic tests.

1998 Thousands die in an earthquake in Afghanistan.

1998 Economic problems in Indonesia: dictator Suharto resigns.

1999 Indonesia: hardline Abdurrahman Wahid is elected president in the first free election since 1955. East Timor votes for independence from Indonesia, leading to massacres and violence UN peace-keeping force intervenes.

1999 Russia sends ground troups into Dagestan and Chechenia, where fighting intensifies. President Yeltsin resigns, but hand-picks his successor, Vladimir Putin.

1999 Pakistani government overthrown by military coup. Benazir Bhutto is imprisoned, allegedly for taking bribes.

1999 Japan's worst nuclear accident: dozens exposed to radiation.

America and Australasia

1996 American scientists warn that global warming has reached record high, introducing possibility of new diseases.

1997 Four month siege of Japanese embassy in Peru by Tupac Amaru guerillas.

1997 Climatic change due to El Niño phenomenon causes extensive damage in South America and southern U.S.A.

Hurricane force winds devastated parts of South and Central America.

1997 Two unmanned NASA spacecraft land on Mars.

Mars, fourth planet from the Sun

1997 Landmark ruling as tobacco industry is forced to pay billions of dollars to lung disease sufferers.

1998 U.S. President Clinton is impeached by Republicans for lying to Congress over his affair with Monica Lewinsky. He is acquitted in 1999.

1998 Hurricane Mitch hits the Caribbean and Central America, killing 9,000 people.

1999 Australians vote to keep British queen as head of state.

31st December 1999 Millions all over the world take part in millennium celebrations, like the firework display (shown below) held in New York, United States of America.

Glossary

amnesty General pardon given by a government for crimes committed. Sometimes granted in an attempt to reach a settlement during a civil war.

annex To join a territory to a larger one by conquering or occupying it.

apartheid South African policy of the separation of races.

aristocracy Government by nobles, or a privileged class.

autocracy Government by a person such as a king, who has unrestricted authority and does not allow any opposition. Government of this kind is described as autocratic.

autonomy Self-government, often limited, granted to a nation or people by a more powerful nation.

Bantu African languages and peoples found between the equator and the Cape of Good Hope.

baptize To immerse a person in water, as part of the initiation ceremony into the Christian Church.

caliph Title given to the successors of Mohammed, rulers of Islamic states. The office or state is called a caliphate.

canonize To declare a person a saint.

capitalism A system in which the means of production (industries, businesses, etc.) are owned by a relatively small group, who provide the investment and take a major share of the profits.

cede To give up or surrender a territory, often as part of the terms of a peace treaty following a war.

charter Document issued by a government, granting certain rights, such as the right to found a colony.

Christendom The people and nations who belong to the Christian Church.

Christianity The religion founded in Palestine by Jesus of Nazareth, known as Jesus Christ.

city-state A state that is made up of a city and its surrounding territory, such as the city-states of Ancient Greece or Italy during the Renaissance.

civil rights Equality in social, economic and political matters.

coalition Temporary alliance between different groups or parties, such as in a government.

collectivization Organization of the ownership of the means of production (factories, farms etc.) into groups, or collectives.

colony A settlement in a country distant from the homeland. A Crown colony is one whose administration is controlled by the King or Queen.

Commonwealth Organization of former member countries of the British empire, with the purpose of mutual co-operation and aid.

communism An ideology mainly based on the ideas of Karl Marx, which advocates a society without social classes or private ownership, in which the means of production (factories and businesses) are owned by the state. In the 20th century, the U.S.S.R and eastern European countries were communist states, as well as China and Cuba, which are still communist today.

Congress The government of the U.S.A., made up of the Senate and the House of Representatives.

coup d'état Sudden overthrow of an existing government by a small group, often army officers.

demilitarization The removal of any soldiers, weapons, etc. from an area.

democracy An ideology which originated in Ancient Greece, meaning "rule by the people".

dependency Territory subject to a nation, to which it is not usually linked geographically.

despot An "absolute" or autocratic ruler, or tyrant, who rules unjustly.

dictator A non-royal autocratic ruler, who imposes his rule by force. The government is called a dictatorship.

dominion The name formerly used for a self-governing colony within the British empire, such as Canada.

ecclesiastical Relating to the Church.

egalitarian System that promotes equality between people.

enlightened despot A despot who tries to govern in the interests of the people, according to the ideals of the Enlightenment, an 18th century philosophical movement, which stressed the importance of reason.

excommunicate To expel a person from the Catholic Church. This is done by the Pope.

fascism A political ideology first developed by Mussolini. A form of government which allows no rival political parties and which controls the lives of its citizens. The Nazi Party in Germany was a fascist party.

federal Relating to a type of government in which power is shared between central government and several regional governments.

guerilla A fighter operating in secret, usually against the government. From the Spanish *guerra*, meaning war.

hegemony Domination of one power or state within a league or federation.

homage Public display of respect to someone, such as a feudal lord.

infallibility Being incapable of error. A principle applied to certain pronouncements by the Pope.

Islam The religion of Muslims, based around the holy book the *Koran*, which teaches that there is only one God and Mohammed is his prophet.

Judaism The religion of the Jewish people, based on the *Old Testament* of the *Bible* and the *Talmud*, with a central belief in one God.

junta Government by a group of army officers, often after a coup d'état.

left-wing Term used to describe any ideology that tends toward socialism or communism.

liberalism Political ideology advocating individual freedom and the idea that governments should interfere as little as possible in people's lives.

mandate Authority given to a country by the League of Nations, which met between 1920 and 1946, to administer another country under its trusteeship.

martial law Rule of law established by military courts, and maintained by the army, in the absence of civil authority.

Marxist Person or government following the teachings of Karl Marx. The belief that actions and institutions are determined by economics, that the struggle between social classes is the instrument of change and that capitalism will eventually be overcome by communism.

medieval Relating to the Middle Ages, a period in European history dating loosely from c. 500-1500.

minority rule Government by a group of people who are different, politically or racially, from a larger group over whom they rule.

monopoly Sole right to trade in a specific product or a specific area.

nationalism Common cultural characteristics, such as race or language, that link groups of people together. It sometimes leads to a movement for national independence, or separation from another ruling state.

nepotism Granting of an official position, or other privilege, to a member of the family, or friend.

nomads People who move continually from place to place.

oligarchy Government by a small group of people, such as in Ancient Greece.

one-party-state Nation that is dominated by the one and only party that is allowed to exist.

papal bull Formal document issued by the Pope.

parliamentary democracy Modern form of democracy, in which representatives elected by the people make decisions on their behalf.

patent Document issued by a government, granting specific rights.

plebiscite Direct vote by the people on an issue of particular importance, such as unification with another state.

pretender Someone who makes a claim to a throne or a title.

privateer Privately-employed soldier, sailor or vessel commissioned for service by a government.

protector Someone who exercises royal authority during the reign of a child, or an ill or unfit monarch.

protectorate Territory largely controlled by, but not annexed to, a more powerful nation.

radical Tending toward extreme or fundamental social, political or economic changes.

regent Ruler of a country during the reign of a child or the absence or incapacity of the monarch.

republic State ruled by representatives of the people, without a king or queen. The first republic was in Ancient Rome.

residency Official house of a British governor in an Indian princedom.

sack Plunder or destruction of a place by an army or mob.

secular Relating to worldly, as opposed to religious, matters.

serf A person with no freedom, who is bound to the land. Found in medieval Europe and pre-revolutionary Russia.

separatist Person or organization that advocates separation from a larger unit.

socialism Ideology that stresses equality of income and wealth, and public (state) ownership of industries (the means of production).

sovereignty Supreme authority or power of a sovereign or state.

state of emergency Crisis during which a government temporarily suspends all the usual rights and liberties of a people.

suffragette A woman who fought a militant campaign for votes for women, especially in Britain at the start of the 20th century.

sultan Supreme ruler of a Muslim state, such as the Ottoman empire.

suzerainty Position of a state exercising a degree of domination over a dependent state.

temporal See **secular**.

terrorist Someone who uses terror (bombing, assassinations, etc.) as a means of political persuasion.

Third World The relatively underdeveloped, unindustrialized countries of Africa, Asia and South America, outside the Eastern (communist) and Western (non-communist) blocs.

tribute Payment made by one nation or people to another, more dominant one, acknowledging submission.

triumvirate Coalition of three rulers, such as Caesar, Crassus and Pompey in Ancient Rome.

tyranny Oppressive and unjust government by a despotic ruler.

ultimatum A final offer by a government or party, in which it insists on certain conditions.

vassal A person or nation in a subordinate relationship to another person or nation.

Prime Ministers and Presidents

PRIME MINISTERS OF GREAT BRITAIN

Party: Conservative (C), Labour (Lab), Liberal (Lib), Conservative-Unionist (CU),
Coalition (Coal), National (N), Tory (T), Whig (W)

1721-1742	(W) Sir Robert Walpole	1834	(Lib) Lord Melbourne	1908-1915	(Lib) Herbert Henry Asquith
1742-1743	(W) Sir Spencer Compton	1834-1835	(C) Sir Robert Peel	1915-1916	(Coal) Herbert Henry Asquith
1743-1754	(W) Henry Pelham	1835-1841	(Lib) Lord Melbourne	1916-1922	(Coal) David Lloyd George
1754-1756	(W) Duke of Newcastle	1841-1846	(C) Sir Robert Peel	1922-1923	(C) Andrew Bonar Law
1756-1757	(W) Duke of Devonshire	1846-1852	(Lib) Lord John Russell	1923-1924	(C) Stanley Baldwin
1757-1762	(W) Duke of Newcastle	1852	(C) Earl of Derby	1924	(Lab) J. Ramsay MacDonald
1762-1763	(T) John Stuart, Earl of Bute	1852-1855	(Lib-Coal) Earl of Aberdeen	1924-1929	(C) Stanley Baldwin
1763-1765	(W) George Grenville	1855-1858	(Lib) Lord Palmerston	1929-1931	(Lab) J. Ramsay MacDonald
1765-1766	(W) Marquis of Rockingham	1858-1859	(C) Earl of Derby	1931-1935	(Nat) J. Ramsay MacDonald
1766-1768	(W) William Pitt the Elder	1859-1865	(Lib) Lord Palmerston	1935-1937	(Nat) Stanley Baldwin
1768-1770	(W) Duke of Grafton	1865-1866	(Lib) Lord John Russell	1937-1940	(Nat) Neville Chamberlain
1770-1782	(T) Lord North	1866-1868	(C) Earl of Derby	1940-1945	(Coal) Sir Winston Churchill
1782-1783	(W) Earl of Shelburne	1868	(C) Benjamin Disraeli	1945-1951	(Lab) Clement Attlee
1783	(Coal) Duke of Portland	1868-1874	(Lib) William Gladstone	1951-1955	(C) Sir Winston Churchill
1783-1801	(T) William Pitt (Younger)	1874-1880	(C) Benjamin Disraeli	1955-1957	(C) Sir Anthony Eden
1801-1804	(T) Henry Addington	1880-1885	(Lib) William Gladstone	1957-1963	(C) Sir Harold Macmillan
1804-1806	(T) William Pitt (Younger)	1885-1886	(C) Marquess of Salisbury	1963-1964	(C) Sir Alec Douglas-Home
1806-1807	(W) Lord Grenville	1886	(Lib) William Gladstone	1964-1970	(Lab) Sir Harold Wilson
1807-1809	(T) Duke of Portland	1886-1892	(CU) Marquess of Salisbury	1970-1974	(C) Sir Edward Heath
1809-1812	(T) Spencer Perceval	1892-1894	(Lib) William Gladstone	1974-1976	(Lab) Sir Harold Wilson
1812-1827	(T) Earl of Liverpool	1894-1895	(Lib) Earl of Rosebery	1976-1979	(Lab) James Callaghan
1827	(T) George Canning	1895-1902	(CU) Marquess of Salisbury	1979-1990	(C) Margaret Thatcher
1827-1828	(T) Viscount Goderich	1902-1905	(C) Arthur James Balfour	1990-1997	(C) John Major
1828-1830	(T) Duke of Wellington	1905-1908	(Lib) Sir H. Campbell-	1997-	(Lab) Tony Blair
1830-1834	(Lib) Earl Grey		Bannerman		

✪ ✪ ✪ ✪ ✪

PRESIDENTS OF U.S.A.

Inauguration date followed by Party: Federation (F), Republican (R), Democrat (D), Whig (W)

1789	(F) George Washington	1732-1799	1861	(R) Abraham Lincoln	1809-1865	1929	(R) Herbert Hoover	1874-1964
1797	(F) John Adams	1735-1826	1865	(R) Andrew Johnson	1808-1875	1933	(D) Franklin Roosevelt	1882-1945
1801	(R) Thomas Jefferson	1743-1826	1869	(R) Ulysses S. Grant	1822-1885	1945	(D) Harry S. Truman	1884-1972
1809	(R) James Madison	1751-1836	1877	(R) Rutherford Hayes	1822-1893	1953	(R) Dwight Eisenhower	1890-1969
1817	(R) James Monroe	1758-1831	1881	(R) James Garfield	1831-1881	1961	(D) John F. Kennedy	1917-1963
1825	(R) John Quincy Adams	1767-1848	1881	(R) Chester Arthur	1830-1886	1963	(D) Lyndon B. Johnson	1908-1973
1829	(D) Andrew Jackson	1767-1845	1885	(D)Grover Cleveland	1837-1908	1969	(R) Richard Nixon	1913-1994
1837	(D) Martin Van Buren	1782-1862	1889	(R) Benjamin Harrison	1833-1901	1974	(R) Gerald Ford	1913-
1841	(W) William Harrison	1773-1841	1893	(D) Grover Cleveland	1837-1908	1977	(D) Jimmy Carter	1924-
1841	(W) John Tyler	1790-1862	1897	(R) William McKinley	1843-1901	1981	(R) Ronald Reagan	1911-
1845	(D) James Knox Polk	1795-1849	1901	(R) Theodore Roosevelt	1858-1919	1989	(R) George Bush	1924-
1849	(W) Zachary Taylor	1784-1850	1909	(R) William Taft	1857-1930	1993	(D) Bill Clinton	1946-
1850	(W) Millard Fillmore	1800-1874	1913	(D) Woodrow Wilson	1856-1924	2001	(R) George W. Bush	1946-
1853	(D) Franklin Pierce	1804-1869	1921	(R) Warren Harding	1865-1923			
1857	(D) James Buchanan	1791-1868	1923	(R) Calvin Coolidge	1872-1933			

PRIME MINISTERS OF CANADA

In 1867 Lower Canada (Quebec), Upper Canada (Ontario), Nova Scotia, and New Brunswick united to form the Dominion of Canada.

Party: Conservative (C), Progressive Conservative (Prog.C), Liberal (Lib), Unionist (UN)

1867-1873 (C) Sir John A. Macdonald
1873-1878 (Lib) Alexander Mackenzie
1878-1891 (C) Sir John A. Macdonald
1891-1892 (C) Sir John J. Abbott
1892-1894 (C) Sir John S. D. Thompson
1894-1896 (C) Sir MacKenzie Bowell
1896 (C) Sir Charles Tupper
1896-1911 (Lib) Sir Wilfred Laurier
1911-1920 (C/UN) Sir Robert L. Borden
1920-1921 (UN) Arthur Meighen
1921-1926 (Lib) W. L. Mackenzie King
1926 (C) Arthur Meighen
1926-1930 (Lib) W. L. Mackenzie King
1930-1935 (C) Richard Bedford Bennett
1935-1948 (Lib) W. L. Mackenzie King
1948-1957 (Lib) Louis St. Laurent
1957-1963 (Prog.C) John G. Diefenbaker
1963-1968 (Lib) Lester B. Pearson
1968-1979 (Lib) Pierre Elliott Trudeau
1979-1980 (Prog.C) Joe Clark
1980-1984 (Lib) Pierre Elliott Trudeau
1984 (Lib) John Turner
1984-1993 (C) Brian Mulroney
1993 (Prog.C) Kim Campbell
1993- (Lib) Jean Chrétien

PRESIDENTS OF EIRE

Party: Fianna Foil (FF), Fine Gael (FG), Labour (Lab), United Ireland (UI)

1938-1945 (No party) Douglas Hyde
1945-1959 (FF) Sean O'Kelly
1959-1973 (FF) Eamon de Valera
1973-1974 (FF) Erskine Childers
1974-1976 (FF) Cearbhall O'Dalaigh
1976-1989 (FF) Patrick John Hillery
1989-1997 (Lab) Mary Robinson
1997- (FF) Mary McAleese

PRIME MINISTERS OF AUSTRALIA

In 1901, the separate British colonies in Australia joined the Commonwealth and became states with a central government.

Party: Free Trade/Protectionist (FT/P), Protectionist (Pro), Labour (Lab), Liberal (Lib), United Australian (UAus), United Country (UC), Nationalist (Nat), Nationalist Country (N/C), Country (Co)

1901-1903 (Pro) Edmund Barton
1903-1904 (Pro) Alfred Deakin
1904 (Lab) John Christian Watson
1904-1905 (FT/P) Sir George H. Reid
1905-1908 (Pro) Alfred Deakin
1908-1909 (Lab) Andrew Fisher
1909-1910 (Pro) Alfred Deakin
1910-1913 (Lab) Andrew Fisher
1913-1914 (Lib) Joseph Cook
1914-1915 (Lab) Andrew Fisher
1915-1923 (Lab/Nat) William M. Hughes
1923-1929 (Nat/Co) Stanley M. Bruce
1929-1932 (Lab) James Henry Scullin
1932-1939 (UAus/Co) Joseph A. Lyons
1939 (April) (UC) Sir Earle Page
1939-1941 (UAus) Sir Robert G. Menzies
1941 (Co) Sir Arthur Wm. Fadden
1941-1945 (Lab) John Joseph Curtin
1945 (Lab) Francis Michael Forde
1945-1949 (Lab) Joseph B. Chifley
1949-1966 (Lib) Robert G. Menzies
1966-1967 (Lib) Harold E. Holt
1967-1968 (Co) John McEwen
1968-1971 (Lib) Sir John Grey Gorton
1971-1972 (Lib) Sir William McMahon
1972-1975 (Lib) Gough Whitlam
1975-1983 (Lab) John Malcom Fraser
1983-1991 (Lab) Bob Hawke
1991-1996 (Lab) Paul Keating
1996- (Lib) John Howard

PRIME MINISTERS OF NEW ZEALAND

From 1856-1907 self-government was granted in New Zealand. In 1907 the country became a dominion.

Party: Liberal (Lib), Labour (Lab), Reform (Ref), United (U), National (Nat)

1906-1912 (Lib) Sir G. Joseph Ward
1912 (Lib) Thomas MacKenzie
1912-1925 (Ref) William F. Massey
1925 (Ref) Sir Francis Bell
1925-1928 (Ref) Joseph G. Coates
1928-1930 (U) Sir Joseph G. Ward
1930-1935 (U) George W. Forbes
1935-1940 (Lab) Michael J. Savage
1940-1949 (Lab) Peter Fraser
1949-1957 (Nat) Sir Sidney G. Holland
1957 (Nat) Sir Keith J. Holyoake
1957-1960 (Lab) Sir Walter Nash
1960-1972 (Nat) Sir Keith J. Holyoake
1972 (Nat) John Ross Marshall
1972-1974 (Lab) Norman E. Kirk
1974 (Lab) Hugh Watt (acting)
1974-1975 (Lab) Sir Wallace Rowling
1975-1984 (Nat) Robert D. Muldoon
1984-1989 (Lab) David R. Lange
1989-1990 (Lab) Geoffrey Palmer
1990 (Lab) Mike Moore
1990-1997 (Nat) Jim Bolger
1997-1999 (Nat) Jenny Shipley
1999- (Lab) Helen Clark

PRIME MINISTERS OF EIRE

1922-1932 (UI) William Cosgrave
1932-1948 (FF) Eamon de Valera
1948-1951 (FG) John Aloysius Costello
1951-1954 (FF) Eamon de Valera
1954-1957 (FG) John Aloysius Costello
1957-1959 (FF) Eamon de Valera
1959-1966 (FF) Sean Lemass
1966-1973 (FF) Jack Lynch
1973-1977 (FG) Liam Cosgrave
1977-1979 (FF) Jack Lynch
1979-1981 (FF) Charles Haughey
1981-1982 (FG) Garrett Fitzgerald
1982 (FF) Charles Haughey
1982-1987 (FG) Garrett Fitzgerald
1987-1992 (FF) Charles Haughey
1992-1994 (FF) Albert Reynolds
1994-1997 (FG) John Bruton
1997- (FF) Bertie Ahern

Kings and Queens

Here are the reign dates of some of the most important monarchies and dynasties of Europe.

KINGS AND QUEENS OF ENGLAND

Saxons	c.500-1066
Normans	1066-1154
Plantagenets	1154-1399
Lancastrians	1399-1461
Yorkists	1461-1485
Tudors	1485-1603
Stuarts	1603-1714
Hanoverians	1714-1910
Windsors	1910-

c.500-802	Rulers of seven kingdoms of England
802-839	Egbert
839-858	Ethelwulf
858-860	Ethelbald
860-866	Ethelbert
866-871	St. Ethelred I
871-899	Alfred the Great
899-925	Edward the Elder
925-939	Athelstan
939-946	Edmund I
946-955	Eadred
955-959	Edwy
959-975	Edgar
975-978	Edward the Martyr
978-1016	Ethelred II "The Unready"
1016	Edmund II "Ironside"
1016-1035	Canute (or Cnut)
1037-1040	Harold I
1040-1042	Harthacnut
1042-1066	Edward the Confessor
1066	Harold II
1066-1087	William I "The Conqueror"
1087-1100	William II
1100-1135	Henry I
1135-1154	Stephen
1135	Matilda declared Queen
1154-1189	Henry II
1189-1199	Richard I
1199-1216	John
1216-1272	Henry III
1272-1307	Edward I
1307-1327	Edward II
1327-1377	Edward III
1377-1399	Richard II
1399-1413	Henry IV
1413-1422	Henry V
1422-1461	Henry VI

1461-1470	Edward IV
1470-1471	Henry VI regained crown
1471-1483	Edward IV regained crown
1483	Edward V
1483-1485	Richard III
1485-1509	Henry VII
1509-1547	Henry VIII
1547-1553	Edward VI
1553	Lady Jane Grey
1553-1558	Mary I
1558-1603	Elizabeth I

KINGS AND QUEENS OF ENGLAND AND SCOTLAND

1603-1625	James I (James VI of Scotland)
1625-1649	Charles I
1649-1660	Britain is ruled as a Commonwealth (1653-1658 Oliver Cromwell is Lord Protector)
1660-1685	Charles II
1685-1688	James II
1689-1694	William III and Mary II
1694-1702	William III reigns alone
1702-1714	Anne

KINGS AND QUEENS OF UNITED KINGDOM

1714-1727	George I
1727-1760	George II
1760-1820	George III
1820-1830	George IV
1830-1837	William IV
1837-1901	Victoria
1901-1910	Edward VII
1910-1936	George V
1936	Edward VIII
1936-1952	George VI
1952-	Elizabeth II

KINGS AND QUEENS OF SCOTLAND

843-860	Kenneth MacAlpin
1005-1034	Malcolm II
1057-1093	Malcolm III
1124-1153	David I
1153-1165	Malcolm IV
1214-1249	Alexander II

1249-1286	Alexander III
1286-1290	Margaret of Norway
1292-1296	John Balliol (removed by Edward I of England)
1306-1329	Robert I "the Bruce"
1329-1371	David II
1371-1390	Robert II
1390-1406	Robert III
1406-1437	James I
1437-1460	James II
1460-1488	James III
1488-1513	James IV
1513-1542	James V
1542-1567	Mary Stuart
1567-1603	James VI (who becomes James I of England, Scotland and Ireland)

FRANKISH KINGDOMS
(includes part of France, Germany, Italy)

Merovingian dynasty	447-751
Carolingian dynasty	751-987

447-458	Merovich
458-481	Childeric I
481-511	Clovis I

(Clovis's kingdom is divided into three. Here are some of the main kings.)

511-558	Childebert I
558-562	Clothaire I
562-566	Caribert
566-584	Chilperic
584-628	Clothaire II
628-637	Dagobert I
637-655	Clovis II
655-668	Clothaire III
668-674	Childeric II
674-691	Thierry III
691-695	Clovis III
695-711	Childebert II
711-716	Dagobert III
716-721	Chilperic II
721-737	Thierry IV

737-743	Interregnum: Charles Martel is governor between 714-741

743-751	Childeric III
751-768	Pepin "The Short"
768-814	Charlemagne (Emperor of the Romans 800-814)
814-840	Louis I
840-877	Charles I "The Bald"

877-879	Louis II "The Stammerer"
879-882	Louis III
882-884	Carloman
884-888	Charles II, "The Fat"
888-898	Odo (Count of Paris)
898-929	Charles III, "The Simple"
929-936	Interregnum
936-954	Louis IV, "The Foreigner"
954-986	Lothaire
986-987	Louis V

KINGS OF FRANCE

Capetians · 987-1328
Valois   1328-1589
Bourbons 1589-1883 (48)

987-996	Hugh Capet
996-1031	Robert II "The Pious"
1031-1060	Henri II
1060-1108	Philippe I
1108-1137	Louis VI "The Grand"
1137-1180	Louis VII "The Young"
1180-1223	Philippe II Augustus
1223-1226	Louis VIII "The Lion"
1226-1270	Louis IX "Saint Louis"
1270-1285	Philippe III "The Strong"
1285-1314	Philippe IV "The Fair"
1314-1316	Louis X
1316	Jean I
1316-1322	Philippe V "The Tall"
1322-1328	Charles IV "The Fair"
1328-1350	Philippe VI
1350-1364	Jean II "The Good"
1364-1380	Charles V "The Wise"
1380-1422	Charles VI
1422-1461	Charles VII "The Victorious"
1461-1483	Louis XI "The Spider"
1483-1498	Charles VIII
1498-1515	Louis XII
1515-1547	François I
1547-1559	Henri II
1159-1560	François II
1560-1574	Charles IX
1574-1589	Henri III
1589-1610	Henri IV
1610-1643	Louis XIII
1643-1715	Louis XIV "The Sun King"
1715-1774	Louis XV
1774-1789	Louis XVI

1789-1804 Revolutionary period:
France is ruled by National Assembly,
National Convention, Directory,
Consulate and then 1st Republic

1804-1814	Napoleon I (Emperor)
1815-1824	Louis XVIII
1824-1830	Charles X
1830-1848	Louis Philippe
1848-1852	2nd Republic
1852-1870	Napoleon III (Emperor)
1870-1940	3rd Republic
1940-1944	German occupation/ Vichy government
1944-1946	Provisional government
1946-1958	4th Republic
1958-	5th Republic

EMPERORS OF THE GERMANS AND OF THE HOLY ROMAN EMPIRE

The coronation of Otto I as
"Holy Roman Emperor of the
German nation" marked a new
stage in medieval thinking. The
emperors saw themselves as
inheriting the old Roman empire
as well as the Christian empire of
Europe. The area they ruled over,
and their degree of control, varied
from period to period, but it
consisted roughly of Germany,
with parts of Austria and Italy.

962-973	Otto I "The Great"
973-983	Otto II
983-1002	Otto III
1002-1024	Henry II "The Saint"
1024-1039	Conrad II
1039-1056	Henry III "The Black"
1056-1106	Henry IV
1106-1125	Henry V
1125-1137	Lothar II of Luxembourg
1138-1152	Conrad III
1152-1190	Frederick I Barbarossa
1190-1197	Henry VI
1198-1215	Otto IV
1198-1208	Philip of Swabia
1220-1250	Frederick II
1250-1254	Conrad IV
1254-1273	Great interregnum
1273-1291	Rudolf I of Habsburg
1292-1298	Adolf I of Nassau
1298-1308	Albert I of Habsburg
1308-1313	Henry VII of Luxembourg
1314-1346	Louis IV of Bavaria
1314-1330	Frederick the Fair (co-regent)
1346-1378	Charles IV of Luxembourg
1378-1400	Wenceslas the Lazy

1400-1410	Rupert of the Palatinate
1410-1437	Sigismund of Luxembourg
1438-1439	Albert II of Habsburg
1440-1493	Frederick III
1493-1519	Maximilian I
1519-1556	Charles V
1558-1564	Ferdinand I
1564-1576	Maximilian II
1576-1612	Rudolf II
1612-1619	Matthias
1619-1637	Ferdinand II
1637-1657	Ferdinand III
1657-1705	Leopold I
1705-1711	Joseph I
1711-1740	Charles VI
1740-1745	Charles VII of Bavaria
1745-1765	Maria Theresa & Francis I
1765-1790	Joseph II
1790-1792	Leopold II
1792-1806	Francis II

(Napoleon abolishes the Holy Roman
Empire in 1806, and Francis II
becomes Emperor of Austria)

EMPERORS OF AUSTRIA

1806-1835	Francis II
1835-1848	Ferdinand I
1848-1916	Francis Joseph I

(The Austrian empire is renamed
Austria-Hungary in 1867)

1916-1918	Charles I
1918-1938	1st Republic
1938-1945	Anschluss
1945-	2nd Republic

RULERS OF GERMANY

Holy Roman Empire   962-1806

Confederation of 39
    German states   1815-1866

Confederation of
Northern Germany   1867-1870

Emperors of Germany   1871-1918

1871-1888	Wilhelm I
1888	Friedrich III
1888-1918	Wilhelm II
1919-1933	Republic of Weimar
1933-1945	3rd Reich
1945-1990	Division of Germany into East and West
1990	Germany united

Kings and Queens

KINGS AND QUEENS OF PORTUGAL

1085-1139	Henrique (Founder of Portugal)
1139-1185	Alfonso I (first king)
1185-1211	Sancho I
1211-1223	Alfonso II
1223-1246	Sancho II
1248-1279	Alfonso III "The Brave"
1279-1325	Dinis "The Farmer"
1325-1357	Alfonso IV
1357-1367	Pedro I
1367-1383	Fernando I
1383-1433	João I
1433-1438	Duarte
1438-1481	Alfonso V
1481-1495	João II
1495-1521	Manuel
1521-1557	João III
1557-1578	Sebastian
1578-1580	Cardinal Henry
1580-1598	Philip I (Philip II of Spain)
1598-1621	Philip II (Philip III of Spain)
1621-1640	Philip III (Philip IV of Spain)
1640-1656	João IV
1656-1667	Alfonso VI
1667-1706	Pedro II
1706-1750	João V
1750-1777	Joseph Emanuel (Power held by statesman Sebastiao José de Carvalho e Mellò)
1777-1816	Maria I
1816-1826	João VI (Ruled in Maria I's name in 1792 after she became insane, becoming regent in 1799)
1826-1834	disputed succession
1834-1853	Maria III & (from 1837) Ferdinand
1853-1861	Pedro V
1861-1889	Luís I
1989-1908	Carlos
1908-1910	Manuel II
1910	Portuguese Republic

KINGS OF ITALY

1861-1878	Victor Emmanuel II
1878-1900	Umberto I
1900-1946	Victor Emmanuel III
1925-1943	Mussolini's dictatorship
1946	Umberto II
1946	Italian Republic

KINGS AND QUEENS OF SPAIN

1492-1516	Isabella of Castile and Ferdinand V of Aragon
1516-1556	Charles I
1556-1598	Phillip II
1598-1621	Philip III
1621-1665	Philip IV
1665-1700	Charles II
1700-1724	Philip V
1724	Louis I
1724-1746	Philip V
1746-1759	Ferdinand VI
1759-1788	Charles III
1788-1808	Charles IV
1808	Ferdinand VII
1808-1813	Joseph Bonaparte
1813-1833	Ferdinand VII
1833-1868	Isabella II
1668-1873	disputed succession
1873-1875	1st Republic
1875-1885	Alphonso XII
1885-1931	Alphonso XIII (overthrown)
1931-1939	2nd Republic & Civil War
1939-1975	Franco's dictatorship
1975-	Juan Carlos (monarchy restored)

TSARS AND TSARINAS OF RUSSIA

1462-1505	Ivan III "The Great"
1505-1533	Vassily III
1533-1584	Ivan IV "The Terrible"
1584-1598	Feodor I
1598-1606	Boris Godunov (Protector)
1603	Feodor II
1603-1606	Grigoriy Otrepieff, usurper, claims to be Dimitri I, son of Ivan IV
1606-1610	Vassily IV (usurper)
1610-1613	Vladyslav (not crowned)

THE ROMANOV DYNASTY

1613-1645	Michael Romanov (elected king)
1645-1676	Alexis
1676-1682	Feodor III
1682-1696	Ivan V and Peter I "The Great" (co-tsars)
1682-1725	Peter I "The Great" (known as "emperor" from 1721)
1725-1727	Catherine I
1727-1730	Peter II
1730-1740	Anna
1740-1741	Anna Leopoldovna (regent for her son Ivan VI)
1741-1762	Elizabeth
1762	Peter III (replaced by his wife Catherine)
1762-1796	Catherine II "The Great"
1796-1801	Paul I
1801-1825	Alexander I
1825-1855	Nicholas I
1855-1881	Alexander II
1881-1894	Alexander III
1894-1917	Nicholas II
1917	Russian Revolution
1922-1991	U.S.S.R (Soviet Union)
1991-	Russian Republic Dissolution of U.S.S.R. into 15 nations

Internet Links

If you have access to the Internet you can visit these Web sites to find out more about world history. For links to the sites, go to the Usborne Quicklinks Web site at **www.usborne-quicklinks.com** and enter the keywords "mini timelines".

Web site 1 Choose any year in the 20th century and read the top news stories, sporting records, scientific advances and lists of the most popular books, films and music of the year.

Web site 2 Find out how science has developed over the years and try out some theories for yourself by playing interactive games.

Web site 3 Listen to recordings of famous speeches in history, such as Martin Luther King Jr.'s "I have a dream" speech, or wander through exhibits based on historical themes.

Web site 4 Try interactive animations, exercises and test-yourself quizzes to discover how key events around the world shaped the 20th century.

Web site 5 Prepare for exams by using practice tests and a question and answer library on a range of history topics.

Web site 6 Uncover the past as you browse a wide selection of games,

animations, video clips, 3-D reconstructions and picture galleries.

Web site 7 Find out how life used to be in Japan, as you take a virtual tour of the city of Edo, now known as Tokyo, and discover more about Japanese culture and traditional art.

Web site 8 Watch the story of the last millennium unfold, as you look at pictures, maps and timelines, outlining the main historical events in each century.

Web site 9 View authentic examples of fashion from around the world and through different periods of history during the last four hundred years.

Web site 10 Find out about the great world explorers and maritime discovery, from ancient times to Captain Cook's 1768 voyage to the South Pacific, and try some fun activities such as making your own globe or compass.

Web site 11 Gain fascinating insights into Chinese culture by searching timelines of Chinese inventions and events in the history of China, which also show what was happening in the rest of the world at the same time.

Web site 12 Take an online journey and explore ancient Egypt, Greece,

Rome, Africa and the Near East, with puzzles to solve and games to play.

Web site 13 Discover more about the history of art by looking at all kinds of historical objects and finding out about the times when they were made.

Web site 14 Find detailed maps, charts and timelines that show how civilization has evolved from prehistoric times to the present day, and explore links to information about the people and events.

Web site 15 Look back at the milestones in space exploration and search an interactive timeline.

Internet safety

The Web sites listed in Usborne Quicklinks are regularly reviewed and updated by Usborne editors. However, the content of a Web site may change at any time and Usborne Publishing is not responsible and does not accept liability for the availability or content of any Web site other than its own, or for any exposure to harmful, offensive, or inaccurate material which may appear on the Web. Usborne Publishing will have no liability for any damage or loss caused by viruses that may be downloaded as a result of browsing the sites it recommends.

When using the Internet, please follow the Internet Safety Guidelines shown on the Usborne Quicklinks Web site.

Index

119

123

Photography credits

b, bottom; m, middle; l, left; r, right; t, top.

Corbis

/Roger Resssmeyer
2-3 Pyramid

/Wolfgang Kaehler
4-5 Minoan dolphins

/Angelo Hornak
18-19 Tree of Jesse stained glass window

/Bettmann
42-43 Spanish map

/Angelo Hornak
52-53 Gosain Narain takes poison

/Hulton-Deutsch Collection
64-65 Storming of the Bastille

/Burstein Collection
76-77 Toulouse Lautrec poster

/Peter Turnley
105 bl Protesters Tiananmen Square

/AFP
106 br Nelson Mandela

/Yann Arthus-Bertrand
107 cl Aerial view of flooded Bangladeshi village

/Sean Aidan; Eye Ubiquitous
108 cl Tony Blair

/Dave Bartruff
108 cr Queen Hatshepsut's mausoleum

/Mike Zens
108-109 b New York fireworks

/Philip Gould
109 tr Palm trees

© **The Channel Tunnel Group Limited**
106 bl Channel Tunnel breakthrough

Hong Kong Tourist Association
109 cl Hong Kong street scene

Illustrated London News
82 cl Karl Marx
84 br Cecil Rhodes
85 tr Abraham Lincoln
86 rc General Gordon

87 lc Indian troops in Burma
90 lc Albert Einstein
92 tl Tsar Nicholas II & family
92 cb Benito Mussolini
92 tr Lawrence of Arabia
93 tl Mao Zedong
93 cl Tokyo after earthquake
94 cl Spanish civil war republican soldiers
95 tl Gandhi
96 cl Churchill, Roosevelt and Stalin
96 cr Rommel's troops after capture

Panos
107 bl Aung Sang Suu Kyi

PETER NEWARK'S MILITARY PICTURES
91 cl Battle of Tsushima

Struan Reid
16 cr Palmyra Roman ruins
29 bl Krak des Chevaliers

Stockbyte/Cadmium
88-89 Spaceman

Turkish Information Office
92 br Mustafa Kemâl "Ataturk"

This edition first published in 2002 by Usborne Publishing Ltd, Usborne House, 83-85 Saffron Hill, London EC1N 8RT, England. www.usborne.com
Copyright © 2002, 2000, 1998 Usborne Publishing Ltd.
The name Usborne and the devices ♀ ⊕ are Trade Marks of Usborne Publishing Ltd. All rights reserved. No part of this publication may be reproduced, stored in a retrieval system, or transmitted in any form or by any means, electronic, mechanical, photocopying, recording or otherwise, without the prior permission of the publisher. First published in America in 2003. UE. Printed in Spain.